Relationship Workbook for Couples

A Guide to Deeper Connection, Intimacy, and Trust for All Couples!

Written By **Smith Douglas**

TABLE OF CONTENTS

Splendid TIP

Achieve something liberal for your accomplice

Unanticipated amazements add feeling to your relationship

Insightful HUMOR

Recognize the estimation of both closeness and impermanent separation

Common Discussion/Negotiation

Ladies (and we think a few men, as well) are biologically customized to react to an infant's needs.

Put your "no" on the rack: Choosing to allow in your partner's love

The five stages that let you take in love

Stage One: Notice That Someone Is Showing You Love

Stage Two: Prepare to Take in Love

Stage Three: Receive Love

Stage Four: Acknowledge That You Feel Loved

Stage Five: Accept That You Are Loved

Make taking in love as a lot of a habit as brushing your teeth.

Love is forgetting to keep track of who's winning.

Say thanks to Your Partner for Those Nice Words and Actions

Take in love at your growing edge

Experience issues loving yourself:

Stage One: Take Responsibility Now, in the Present, for Carrying Around a Damaged Bucket

Stage Two: Gather the Equipment You'll Need to Fix Your Bucket

Feeling confident that I merit loving

Stage Three: Fix the Bucket

The spiritual parts of taking in your partner's love

The Expression of Intimacy

For Premarital Couples:

For Married Couples:

CHAPTER 1

How to Say I Love You

Develop Positive Habit of Saying I Love You?

The objective of this exercise is to assist you with developing the positive habit of stating "I love you" to your partner a few times each day. It sounds sufficiently simple, isn't that right? All things considered, "I love you" is a simple declarative sentence consisting of three short words. In any case, individuals are experts at turning something simple into something painful. We make life complicated, especially with regards to relationships. We make inner turmoil by asking questions like "Would it be a good idea for me to disclose to her I love her?"; "Will he reveal to me he loves me if I state it first?"; "I'd like to state 'I love you,' yet I don't have the foggiest idea how"; and "Yet don't you need to feel loving to state 'I love you truly'?"

Disregard such stuff. Saying "I love you" doesn't need to be com-

7

plicated, confusing, or painful. You simply state it. At that point, you state it again what's more, again. The more regularly you tell your partner that you love him or her, the easier it gets. In the end, you build up a positive habit. That is when saying "I love you" turns into a consistent in your relationship. Also, at exactly that point, when the two partners state "I love you" to one another consistently, do they have a sense of security with one another. Rules and regulations list for developing the positive habit of routinely saying "I love you" to your partner.

What to Do:

1) Concerning saying "I love you," quality is outstanding, anyway, there is no substitute for quantity. Continue saying "I love you" until it ends up being healthy and pleasing.

2) Push through any squares or hesitations you have about saying "I love you." Shyness, reluctance, fear of rejection, fear

of vulnerability, fatigue, anxiety, depression—these emotions are generally genuine and painful. In any case, don't let them keep you from saying the most important thing you can ever state to another person.

3)   Say "I love you" on any occasion, when you are feeling irritated, bugged, irritated, or irritated disagreement is an extraordinary strategy to diminish tension and comfort both yourself and your partner that no conflict will wreck your love.

4)   For a while, monitor how regularly every day you state "I love you." Be a scientist; assemble information. Continuously end, make a note, mental or written, of how much of the time you said "I love you" to your partner. If it was under three, ask yourself what turned out gravely that day so you can reveal specific improvements tomorrow.

5)   Listen to yourself as you state "I love you" and notice how it feels. Concentrate on how you state "I love you" and how you feel as you state it. Okay, have the option to declaration? Do you feel free? Pleasing?

6)   Sneak in a couple "I love you" in startling situations. There is no horrendous time to state "I love you." Add a little carefree nature to your routine by throwing in an "I love you" while making a shopping list, while entertaining organization, or while washing dishes after a blowout.

7)   When in question, decide to state "I love you," don't hesitate to state it. Why not? The risk of something terrible happening is little, and the likelihood of something extraordinary occurring is high. It usually's worth the risk, especially when you are training yourself to state "I love you" consistently.

8) Fantastic method to fluctuate your routine while helping your brain become acclimated to professing your love. "I've gone to the store. I'll be back by 1:00. I love you."

9) Always end your calls with "I love you." If you make this a ritual, each telephone conversation will finish strong.

What not to DO:

1) Ever expect that your partner doesn't have to hear the words "I love you." The individual in question needs to hear those words. Everyone does.

2) Wait until your partner says it first. This is a tremendous mistake since you're giving all the control to your partner. Besides, "I love you, as well" isn't as robust as "I love you."

3) Insist that your partner repay the praise, or keep track of who's winning of how frequently undoubtedly incredible when you receive an "I love you" each time you give one. Yet, don't make that a condition or an interest. State "I love you" to your partner since it's a beautiful gift to give without expecting a gift consequently. Instead of a Christmas gift trade.

4) Keep in mind; the objective is to build up a positive habit. Habits just create with repetition. That is the reason saying "I love you" three times a day is so important.

5) Wait until the perfect or immaculate time. The right time is right at this point. The more you wait, and the more conditions you place on saying "I love you," the more uncertain

you are ever to state it.

6)   Think that saying "I love you" is just "genuine" if it is done unexpectedly. Saying "I love you" tallies in any event, when you need to think about it. It checks in any event when it doesn't fall into place easily.

7)   Expect magic or miracles. Saying "I love you" won't resolve every one of your conflicts. Be that as it may, saying "I love you" creates trust, compatibility, and care that will assist you with lovingly discussing your conflicts.

8)   Automatically associate saying "I love you" with sex. Be mindful so as not to state these words just when you're try-ing to lure your partner. "I love you" is not equivalent to "I need you."

9)   Stop practising until you've built up a firm habit of saying "I love you." Try not to take an "Alright, I get the idea, so I don't need to continue practising" attitude following a few days. It requires some investment to build up settle on a con-scious decision to state them.

Saying I Love You in Different Manners:

The expression "I love you" is incredible. Implies numerous things, for example:

1)   You are special.

2)   You give meaning to my life. I think of you frequently.

3)   I need to fulfil to you. You are a magnificent friend.

Be that as it may, merely translating "I love you" into every one of these expressions. Valid, every aspect might shimmer and shine all alone, yet you need to take a gander at the entire jewel to appreciate it completely. "I love you" is imperative to the point that you should state those accurate words, plainly and distinctly, to your partner. There is no substitute.

Savvy TIP:

Notice how one second is different from another, even though the words remain the equivalent. These two exercises will support both you and your partner feel the full intensity of the expression "I love you."
For the first exercise, kindly do the following:

1.   Find two agreeable chairs and position yourselves so you can take a gander at one another and look.

2.   Decide who will go first. You'll both get a turn.

3.   The first individual says gradually, "I love you," noticing his or her feelings. The other individual takes in those words without remark, at that point stops for a few seconds.

4.   The first individual continues to state "I love you" nine additional times, pausing after each time for a few seconds with the goal that the two partners can notice their feelings.

5.   Neither partner must include any additional words. The quality of "I love you" will just be diluted by "Truly, I do"; "Do you believe me?"; "I realize you do, etc.

The individual can be your partner, an old buddy, a parent—any individual who is deserving of your love (i.e., no old lover with whom you are hoping to reunite). Rafael loves Miranda. Be that as it may, he never advises her so. Why? Since he experienced childhood in a family in which men don't communicate any emotion aside from outrage. Indeed, even now, in his thirties, he thinks he'd be giggled at if anyone at any point heard him proclaim his love. Shelby loves Aaron. In any case, she remains quiet about that information.

Individuals have a wide range of explanations behind not saying "I love you." They, for the most part, appear as, "Something terrible will occur if I state that." The unfortunate outcome will originate from their partner, family individuals, or the general community. As it were, they expect some type of punishment for saying "I love you." Now, occasionally they might be right. Sometimes one's partner reacts to "I love you" with the ugliness ("Well, I don't love you") or others do ridicule the speaker ("Oh, Rafael's going delicate"). However, nothing awful would happen a large portion of the times individuals prevent themselves from stating "I love you." Useful things typically follow from saying those words: embraces, smiles, kind words back.

So then what truly shields a great many people from saying "I love you"? The appropriate response is old, negative, irrational considerations. For instance, Rafael is convinced that individuals will snicker at him if he says he loves Miranda. In any case, what individuals? What's more, for what reason would that stop him when it's merely both of them at home talking with one another? Furthermore, where did Shelby think of the idea that her saying "I love you" to Aaron gives him power?

Quite a while back, a comic book character said, "We have met the adversary, and he is us." That's actually what we're saying here. Shields you from saying "I love you" is you. Cognitive therapists name considerations like Rafael's and Shelby's "irrational." But how about we call them "cold contemplations" here. A virus thought is any idea you have that discourages you from saying something loving, caring, or helpful to your partner. The opposite of cold contemplations is "warm musings." A warm idea is any idea you have that urges you to state something loving, caring, or helpful to your partner. The idea, at that point, is to kick out the cool contemplations from your brain while adding some warm musings. This substitution procedure will help you both state "I love you" all the more frequently and feel good while saying it. You will need to make three basic strides in request to substitute warm musings for cold ones.

Getting Started and Keep Going:

We discussed three squares to intimacy in the last exercise. Dismissiveness drives individuals to avoid cosy relationships inside and out for taking consideration of themselves. The expression "I love you" frequently appears to be futile and even a sign of shortcoming to the dismissed. Preoccupation puts the attention on the other individual the objective is to make one's partner express his or her love. Mean-while, frightfulness makes individuals retreat from all types of intimacy since they become excessively terrified of rejection to risk involvement.

Luckily, individuals are not stuck in one connection style until the end of time. Indeed, inquire about has demonstrated that individuals are likely to advance toward becoming more secure after some time than dismissive, preoccupied, or frightful. What's more, secure is an incredible spot to be regarding. Anyway, if you aren't quite there yet (or need to have a sense of safety in your love all the more frequently), what would you be able to do? The appropriate response lies in this story advised to Ron by an educator he had years back. This man was a specialist in behaviour modification techniques for couples. He was superb at helping partners grow all the more loving and caring behaviours. Be that as it may, this educator had a complaint. He thought that it was a lot easier to get individuals to consent to do the dishes three times per week than to get them to consent to tell their partner "I love you."

The explanation, he said, was that numerous individuals believed an expression like "I love you" ought to be spoken unexpectedly consistently. Planning and committing to state "I love you" five times every day to their partner would feel fake and insincere to these individuals. They needed to wait until they genuinely wanted to state it before they did. Indeed, that hesitance flabbergasted and disappointed Ron's instructor. He contended that an individual could always wait to be inspired to state.

We think that instructor is right. The more regularly you tell your partner you love him or her, the easier it will turn into. What doesn't get more comfortable with practice? Besides, by stating your love, you are helping both yourself and your partner become increasingly dismissive-ness, preoccupation, and dreadfulness. Yet, shouldn't something be said about spontaneity? Shouldn't that have a spot? Certainly. Also, it will. After you practice saying "I love you," however, not previously. That is because the more you practice saying "I love you," the easier it will get, and once it gets easier to state, it will likewise turn out to be increasingly unconstrained. Ask yourself, for instance, who is bound to decide to take a five-mile bike ride suddenly—somebody who hops on a bike possibly twice per year or somebody who rides consistently?

How about we handle another objection to usually always if you state it five times per day instead of saving it for snapshots of particular closeness. All things considered; we think that is off-base. Indeed, we believe that you will mean it increasingly more when you do educate your partner much of the time concerning your love. Think about it this way. There are two listeners each time you state "I love you" for all to hear your partner and yourself. Your brain hears you talk that magic expression. It hears you affirm your love. Imagine your brain saying to itself, "Gracious,

I'm saying I love him [her], so I surmise I do."

Finally, we're not suggesting you counterfeit feelings of love here. Simply since we believe you truly love your partner. So put some emotion into your words. Change your manner of speaking. Have a ton of fun with this experiment. However, whatever you do, continue saying "I love you" so you become progressively alright with that expression.

There's a simple exercise in so much discussion. You need to begin saying "I love you." You need to continue saying "I love you." You need to practice saying "I love you." That's the ideal approach to build and keep love in your life. We're going to expect now that you need to increase the number of times you state "I love you" to your partner. If along these lines, there are two different ways to do it.

Scientific Approach:

Pick two days per week (one weekday, one end of the weekday) to gather your "I love you" baseline information. That implies no-ticing how regularly you tell your partner you love him or her before you begin increasing the number. Try not to think about adding to this number yet. The idea is to get a smart thought of how frequently you, for the most part, say "I love you." Whatever the number, regardless of whether it's zero or twelve, you may still need to increase it. The very first moment (weekday): what number times did you say "I love you" to your partner?

Day Two (weekend day): what number times did you say "I love you" to your partner? Set an objective, for example, saying "I love you" to your partner, at any rate, three times per day on weekdays and in any event six times per day on ends of the week.

Explore Non-Verbal ways to say I Love You:

Yolanda discloses to her partner, Jermaine, "I love you." However, she talks in a monotone, reclines, dismisses, and has all the earmarks of being depleted. Her verbal message is "I love you." But her nonverbal message is "I don't commonly. Indeed, if you're like a considerable number of individuals, the appropriate reaction is the nonverbal message. Study after an examination has exhibited a simple truth: when individuals in this manner, guarantee your nonverbal message coordinates your words. The expression "nonverbal communication" implies various things, mainly:

1)   Vocalisms (delicate to the boisterous way of speaking, monotone to the varied state of mind, etc.)

2)   Touch (delicate to firm)

3)   Body position and advancement (leaning toward to leaning perpetually, completely still to continually active)

4)   Eye contact (none to consistent and direct)

Here's a simple equation for making sure your "I love you" message goes over loud and clear on all channels:
(1) express the words unmistakably and directly
(2) talk in a quiet way of speaking
(3) make direct and "delicate" (not glaring) eye to eye connection
(4) lean toward your partner
(5) (sometimes) contact or hold your partner softly.

By and by, a couple of individuals have an easier time at this than others. If you have a Secure connection style or if you are usually outgoing or experienced childhood in a demonstrative family, chances are quite adequate that your non-verbal communication is unconstrained, productive, and varied. On the other hand, if your connection style is Dismissive or Fearful, or if you are introverted usually or experienced childhood in a no demonstrative family unit, your non-verbal communication might be quieted. Whatever your situation, in any case, it's vital that you communicate as the need ought to arise to your partner. So, recollect the recipe above as you talk. In any case, sometimes you might need to communicate your love to your partner without using any words at all. Here are two or three ways to deal with do that, starting with the most direct.

1) Mouth the words "I love you" from over the room.

2) Use nonverbal funniness: grab your chest and fall over in a loving swoon; draw a heart on the heated washroom mirror.

3) Just look at your partner with a delicate, loving look.

4) Listen to your partner, just as hearing his or her words were the most critical thing you could ever do.

5) Notice the little things that unwind, comfort, or quiet your partner and offer them when required. A timely cup of tea, a grasp, a warm spread, turning the lights on so the individual in question can see better after some time these caring demonstrations will become associated with love.

Use Creativity, Humor and Imagination:

There is something ridiculous about being in love. Loving someone is romantic, silly, exciting, ridiculous, foolish, happy, pleasurable, bittersweet, weird, and extraordinary—consistently all simultaneously. A dangerous thing? Why not toy with the idea of love, exploring some lighter approaches to manage tell your partner the total you give it a misgiving?

That is the spot creativity, cleverness require a gigantic measure of stressful work or cash. You will likely need to put aside some time to outfit your imagination, nevertheless. You'll likewise need to think about what kind of play claims to your partner. You'll require your partner to feel enjoyably surprised and a little giggly, not stunned or ungainly, by your creative undertakings.

Sometimes little things work extraordinary. For instance, you could simply put a sweet note in your partner's movement sack or briefcase. Or on the other hand, pick up a favourited sweet as an unexpected treat. For any situation, possibly you'd be happy to go a bit further, not far-evacuated of creativity. That calls for thinking outside the case. Stance yourself this inquiry: How might I have the option to tell my partner I love him [her] in surprising habits? Your immediate objective ought to be to surprise your partner magnificently. Longer-term, the objective is to keep the love between you feeling new, light-hearted, blissful, and unconstrained.

Here are a few ways you could experiment.

What number of sorts of voices might you have the option to use to state "I love you"? Shouldn't something be said

A Donald Duck quack

A phone receptionist voice A gathering advertiser's call

What kind of physical progressions could go with saying "I love you"? Here are a few possibilities.

Falling over on the floor Kneeling

Standing on your head Arms outstretched

Pretending to hold a microphone Dancing

Jumping all over Hopping

Waddling

Where might you have the option to state "I love you"? Think of spots and situations you would not typically associate with saying "I love you" and a while later state it for any situation.

Praise enables your partner to feel loved

We've done a great deal of marriage counselling, and one thing we've noticed is that upset couples invest more energy criticizing each other than saying anything helpful. Their relationships have step by step gravitated toward assault and guard, shaming, hostility, negativity, and disrespect.

You may as of now be thinking to yourself that individuals see what they are looking for. What's more, you're entirely right. That implies we'll begin seeing all the greater in our partners precisely to the degree that we train ourselves to search for the great. You may likewise be thinking that you get what you react to. Furthermore, again you are right. Individuals who remark exclusively on their partner's flaws are encouraging their partners to deteriorate instead of wager ter. For instance, if you let me know again and again how messy I am, I can nearly promise you that I will get sloppier. Then again, if you focus on the times I tidy up around the house and reveal to me that you appreciate my endeavours, odds are I will keep picking things up.

Individuals should be praised. Your partner should be praised. It makes a difference him or her vibe acknowledged, regarded, needed, and capable. So, ensure that you give praise at any rate four or five times for each critical comment.

If you originate from a family in which praise was only here and there given, it probably doesn't feel normal to give praise to anybody, including your partner. Be that as it may, you definitely can become familiar with this skill. What's more, if you do, your partner will in all likelihood, feel progressively models we give have to do with your relationship.

Deeds. The beautiful things your partner improves. Supper, painting the wardrobe, training the canine . . .

Exertion. The vitality your partner consumes for your relationship. You are taking additional time to be with you, reading this book, working so hard, genuinely listening to you . . .

Insightfulness. The unique ways your partner demonstrates caring to you and others. Little things like bringing you some tea, noticing when you're feeling blue, writing you a special note . . .

Creativity. The fun-loving activities or new ideas your partner thinks of that help keep your relationship alive. A surprise gift, a silly joke, a provocative wink, an idea for another leisure activity or spot to go together . . .

Generosity. The manners in which your partner leaves his or her approach to show caring. You are staying up with the kids when you're excessively tired, asking about your previous day talking about his or her own, performing demonstrations of kindness . . .

Appearance. The uniquely beautiful parts of your partner's style and appearance. His or her excellent armband, beautiful eyes, superb smile, incredible looking coat . . .

Individuality. Select parts of your partner's character and individual it that stick out. His or her genuineness, caring, intelligence, thoughtfulness, quality, optimism, perkiness, tenderness...

Giving praise is a brilliant thing. In any case, we need to caution you against making two fundamental mistakes.

1.   Don't ever follow praise with the word at the same time, as in "Sal; I liked making love with you this morning, however..." That word, however, consistently declares that you are going to express something critical to your partner. The following praise with criticism is like following a kiss with a punch in the nose.

2.   Don't expect or request to receive praise from the individual you praise. Make your praise a gift that accompanies no hidden obligations.

Write a love letter to your partner

For what reason do such a large number of couples falling in love trade love letters? There are numerous ways:

1)   Writing encourages them to think about what they genuinely like about one another.

2)   Writing brings out their romantic side.

3)   Writing encourages them to feel associated with one another in any event when they are separated.

4)   Writing encourages them to tell their partners what their identity is and how they arrived in such a state.

5)   Writing love letters is a method for saying "I love you" that just feels better.

6) Receiving love letters consoles them that their partners are thinking about them.

Love letters step by step transform into practical little notes: "Nectar, if you don't mind picking up bread and milk in transit home tonight." Our suggestion is sufficiently simple. Set aside the effort to write your partner a love letter at any rate once every month. No, it doesn't need to be ten pages in length. A few will do fine and dandy. A little soft, deepest desires, and your apprehensions and worries as opposed to about your pension, the children's contentions, or your lower back pain.

Most likely, the hardest thing about writing a love letter, if you haven't written one for some time, is getting begun. It might assist you with thinking of writing a love letter like getting prepared to concoct a particularly delicious dish. First, you gather your necessary instruments: pen, paper, and whatnot. At that point, you assemble your centre humour, a great deal of warmth, and, generally significant, your style of sharing the love. Simply recollect as you plan your dish that the objective is to make a feast that both you and your partner find delicious. So, ensure you toss in certain words and contemplations that will be particularly pleasing to your partner. Here's the place we come in. We'll gracefully a portion of the essential ingredients for your letter, in the type of suggestions about what you might need to include. Every ingredient is trailed by a model. Realize, however, that you are the culinary expert responsible for this particular dining experience. Utilize any or the entirety of the ingredients we offer, selecting those that assist you with besting express your love for your partner. Include or take away as you like. Write the letter in your style.

Try not to stress over getting it excellent. Simply write.

Proposed Ingredients for a Love Letter

1) That you like how your partner communicates for himself or herself ("You state what you think so obviously")

2) That you still pick your partner ("Of the considerable number of individuals on the planet, I need you most")

3) How lucky you are to have made a life together ("You've made my reality complete")

4) What you've gained from your partner ("I've figured out how to think about others from you")

5) How you've given your partner access to your life ("Only you realize that I am afraid of individuals")

6) That your love is special ("I never figured I could be this much in love with anybody")

7) That you will be valid and faithful ("I need to be with you the remainder of my life")

8) That you will support your partner ("I realize you love blossoms, so how about we plant a nursery")

9) That your partner matters to ("You mean such a great amount to me")

10) How your partner's love solaces you ("I feel quiet and serene around you")

11) Your appreciation of your partner's comical inclination ("You make me smile")

12) That you think of your partner frequently ("I find myself thinking of you constantly")

So, have you made your selections? Which items from the list would you like to include in your love letter? We propose you pick in any event five and perceive how that goes. Experiment with these ingredients for some time. At that point, if you need to continue writing, select another five. Try not to toss in a lot of stuff, however. Generally write another letter in a long time using a couple of more ingredients from the list.

Reclaim Your Relationship

Be mindful to avoid all criticism or negativity. Try not to request that your partner change in any manner. Coincidentally, this is not a no-send letter. You'll need to hand-deliver your letter to your partner, or possibly put it in a particular spot for him or her to discover while you're away. The majority of the exercises in this book are intended to assist peruses with learning approaches to state and do beneficial things for their partners. In any case, we needed to include in any event one exercise on what not to state and do. That is because, as you prob-capably know from your own experience, even one particularly inconsiderate, insensitive, or gutless upheaval can severely harm a relationship.

Moreover, you can't merely offset one frightful remark with one nice remark. Individuals simply give more consideration to terrible stuff than great. That is one explanation the marriage analyst John Gottman suggests a ratio of in any event five praising remarks for each critical one. In any case, if it takes five positive proclamations to compensate for one negative remark, at that point doesn't it bode well to do whatever it takes not to offer that terrible remark in the first spot? Solid relationships rely upon trust just as love. Also, one of the most important territories in which trust creates fixates on this expression: "I know precisely how to hurt you. However, I won't."

This is what we mean. Let's assume you've been going out with somebody for a quarter of a year. At this point, your partner has started to reveal your things. Maybe the individual was mishandled as a child. Perhaps his or her first relationship the words you express today ought to be delicate and delicate . . . for tomorrow you may need to eat them finished bitterly. Possibly the person furtively can't stand a sibling or a sister. The point is that your new partner is slowly feeding you information that you could use against him or her. If you're learning all that in the first hardly any months, imagine the amount you'll know the following three years. You were following thirty-three years.

You are most likely likewise giving your partner information about yourself. That implies you are progressively becoming increasingly defenceless, so your partner is equipped for hurting you, as well. Things are going admirably among you. In any case, at that point comes an immense contention about cash or spending enough time with one another or sex. You're furious with your partner, and the person in question isn't content with you, either. By then, every one of you has a point of view that goes like this:

a.   I'm incredibly frantic at you.

b.   I'm so frantic that piece of me urgently needs to state or accomplish something that will cause you to feel terrible.

c.   I'm enticed, yet would it be advisable for me too?

And afterwards, the lethal mistake: Sure, why not? I may pay for this later, however, right now I'll get that blow in. In any case, what to state? Goodness, yes. Presently I know. You are sensitive about your weight [your intelligence, your competence]. That is the place I'll strike: "Your fat [stupid, incompetent]. There. You did it. You are just prevailing with regards to harming your partner, your relationship, and presumably yourself. In any case, it sure felt useful for a minute we do have a choice, however. We should play in this scene again. However, this time revise it a little.

a.   I'm extremely troubled at you.

b.   I'm so distracted that piece of me urgently needs to state or accomplish something that will cause you to feel terrible.

c.   I'm enticed, however, would it be advisable for me too?

d.   No; as much as I need to insult you right presently, I'm not going to do it. That is not what love is about.

e.   Instead, I'll escape for a couple of moments until I can quiet down or I'll say something caring and keen to move beyond the annoyance.

Choosing not to hurt your partner

Presently, that demonstration of nonaggression took fearlessness, character, and control. It wasn't simple since you were so furious, your fight-or-flight instincts had been activated. Moreover, in all probability, no one will ever realize what you just decided not to do. Be that as it may, you will know.

Why settle on that choice not to assault? There are a few valid justifications. First, you'll most likely like yourself. You dealt with that situation as a grown-up, dignity and restraint. Second, you'll avoid feeling guilty about harming somebody you love. All things considered; individuals don't get into relationships just to have somebody to slam around. Loving somebody implies helping him or her vibe great, not awful. Third, your choice not to go for the jugular makes it far more outlandish that your partner will go for yours. Finally, you'll never resolve any conflicts by attacking each other's character and personality. If you plan to settle that issue about finances or to spend time with one another or sex, you should avoid saying things that ensure your partner will get defensive.

CHAPTER 2

Making Time with your Partner

We accept that two customs of marriage exist together in America (and prob-competently in numerous nations). From one perspective, we have to work outstandingly with our accomplice: the old term "helpmeet" applies here, which we'll change to "right hand." In a well-working marriage, the accomplices resemble two horses hitched to a large truck. Together, if they work agreeably, they can pull that truck far. In any case, we in like manner needs our accomplice to be our dearest companion: someone we can speak with about anything, play with, and all-around appreciate. While the assistant portrayal is two horses pulling a truck, the dearest companion model is progressively similar to two people clasping hands strolling one next to the other down the lifestyle.

Some of the time we meet couples in marriage mentoring, whose primary problem is that one of them accepts only in the accomplice model while the other is attached to the dearest companion thought. The associate benefactor thinks, "Living, all by itself, is a struggle. There's continually a lot to finish. The house must be painted. The children ought to be dealt with. I should have help with so much stuff, or I'll fall to pieces." This person's central objection is that their accomplice doesn't do what's required, doesn't pass on full weight. The most discernibly horrendous thing the assistant individual can call someone is "unconcerned."

Splendid TIP

Give your accomplice two red roses, each with a note. The central note says "For the one I love," Additionally, the second "For my dearest companion." "I didn't get into this relationship essentially to work and work and work. I need feeling, important discussions, and closeness. I need my accomplice to unveil to me everything, and I have to do similarly." The dearest companion person's most exceedingly terrible affront is that someone is "far off," which shows the sum the person being referred to values closeness. Before proceeding, we ought to see how you feel about these two thoughts.

To start with, rate the significance to you of all of the accompanying two statements with a number someplace in the scope of 0 and 10, with 0 signifying "No, that isn't what I need in any way shape or form" and ten signifying "Totally, that is what I most need throughout everyday life." Make sure you put down what you need, not what you figure you should put down. Ask with regards to whether your answers reflect the regular choices you make about your relationship.

1.   More than everything else, I need my accomplice in life to be my helpmate.

2.   More than everything else, I need my accomplice in life to be my dearest companion.

If you are starting at now seeing someone, would be perfect on the off chance that you in like manner, consider how your partner may score those proportionate two sentences.

For you to talk about your answers with your accomplice if that is conceivable. Guarantee that the target of your conversation is recognizance, not influence. You won't win concerning persuading your accomplice to change their characteristics, and convictions about serious relationships don't too Endeavor. Regardless, an incredible conversation about your separate needs may help you with discovering ways for all of you to feel continuously cherished and acknowledged. All things considered; we adults can do something very similar for our partners. Your partner in life can assist you with feeling protected, warm, and, generally meaningful, loved when you are worried, hurting, angry, or dismal, or when you have lost confidence in yourself—however just if you let him or she do that for you. Perhaps at those times, you feel unlovable, yet that doesn't mean your partner needs to concur. The person in question realizes you merit loving. All things considered; your partner has decided to be your partner for some valid justifications. You've likely heard these sayings: "You can't give love to other people if you don't love yourself" and "You can just take in another's love to the degree you love yourself." There must be some fact to them, or individuals wouldn't rehash them as regularly as they do. Indeed, the young lady who reacts to her lover's "I love you" with "Goodness, how right? I do not merit loving" is taking in love just to the degree that she loves herself. Her lover's words make what's called cognitive dissonance between what she believes about herself ("I am unlovable") and what she hears ("You are loved"). A few people do believe they are unlovable. They may venture to such an extreme as to believe they are God's mistake—a complete failure of being. If you are like that, you will need to accomplish some close to homework so you can take in the love of the individuals around you. See our book Letting Go of Shame connect the feeling of being unlovable with the idea of disgrace. Notwithstanding, it would be a big mistake for you, or anyone using this book, to wait until you are "sound" and self-loving before taking in another's love. That is because taking in another's love makes feelings of self-esteem and self-esteem inside you. Here's a typical model. One evening Mary is feeling particularly terrible about herself. She appears to have spoiled everything she's tried today: she did severely on a test at school, she committed a grave error at work, her kids disclosed to her she was mean since she wouldn't let them out of their errands, lastly, just to fill her heart with joy far and away more terrible, she broke one of her favourited espresso cups, spilling hot espresso all over her shirt all the while. Presently in strolls her partner, Charlie. "Hi," he says. "How's it hanging with you?" Mary dissolves into tears. "Terrible," she replies and enlightens him regarding her day. "Well," Charlie reacts, "I'm tragic for you that all that occurred. In any case, you realize I love you. Would I be able to give you an embrace?" So now what are Mary's options? Accomplices in every relationship must arrange the distinctions they have here. For example, chances are you will encounter issues in any occasion occasionally on the off chance that you rate the significance of your accomplice's your dearest companion an eight and a right hand a two while your accomplice rates the significance of your being their dearest companion a three and their assistant a 7. You generally need someone you can work alongside while your accomplice needs much increasingly an ideal accomplice.

Nevertheless, review this: being someone's helper or dearest companion is the two unique methods for indicating love. Neither one of the ways is for each situation better than the other. You and your accomplice don't have to pick between these two distinct methods for demonstrating love considering the way that a caring relationship flourishes with the two segments. It positively is critical to orchestrating that truck. You complete more that way. Also, genuinely, by all strategies, we should turn out to be dearest companions while we're pulling that truck. We should even make a point to unfasten it now and again enough to have a tremendous amount of fun together. Alternating being associates and dearest companions can make your relationship sparkle with adoration.

Listen with love

"You know when I most feel loved? It's the point at which my partner quits everything, sits down, and truly listens to me. That is the point at which I feel critical to him [her]." How prominent is the announcement above for you? For your partner? Probably the most grounded complaint individuals make in marriage counselling is that their partner doesn't listen to them. They don't typically imply that the other per-child ignores them, however. What they mean is that they don't get the feeling that their partner is paying loving attention to them. They need their partner to listen with his or her ears, mind, and heart. At the point when that doesn't occur, they feel distant from their partner. However, when they do detect that their partner is listening to that way, they feel profoundly cherished. Simply expressed, perhaps the most ideal approaches to show your partner your caring is to listen with love. Listening with love takes concentration, vitality, and a willingness to set your contemplations aside for later for some time. Here are a few suggestions for listening with love.

1.   Invite your partner to talk so you can listen with love. Listening with love is a skill. You will show signs of improvement at it the more you practice. So how would you get opportunities to practice? By asking your partner at any rate once every day to discuss things that issue to him or her and afterwards making it your objective to listen with love.

2.   Put aside any distractions that might shield you from listening. Mood killer the TV. Advise the kids to play without anyone else for a while. Similarly, as necessary, put aside any musings or worries that might distract you from paying complete consideration to your partner. Remind yourself that you would need your partner to completely take care of you if you had something important on your mind.

3.   Take a positive attitude when your partner begins speaking. Try not to get defensive. Try not to be critical. You can't both listen with love and criticize your partner. Instead, disclose to yourself that your partner is an intelligent, attentive individual whose ideas are worth listening to.

4.   Let your partner realize you are listening nonverbally through eye con-respect, contact, gestures, and facial expres-

sions. Listening with love is a full-body activity. You have to take a gander at your partner (with loving, not glaring, eyes). Occasional delicate contacts pass on the message "I'm here with you; continue talking" with-out distracting your partner. Gestures state "Truly, I hear you" just as "I concur with you." Facial expressions are especially important if you tend to listen with an empty look. Your partner may peruse a vague expression to signify "I'm not so much interested in what you're saying," so ensure you let your face demonstrate some reaction to your partner's words.

5. Keep the attention on your partner as opposed to talking about yourself. Listening with love is not typical to and for conversation. Regularly, one individual discussion for some time about himself or herself and afterwards different dominates. Be that as it may, in listening with love, you have to maintain the attention on your partner. Your primary responsibility is to draw out your partner to keep him or her talking. So, don't switch the topic to yourself. Most importantly, don't assume control over the conversation with the goal that your partner thinks, "Hello, I began to tell about myself, and now everything we're doing is talking about him [her]."

6. Ask questions that urge your partner to continue sharing his or her contemplations and feelings. "What's your opinion about that?" "What's generally important to you about what you just said?" "OK, reveal to me progressively about that?" "How might you get that going?" "What do you need?" Note: Be cautious about asking "why questions" as in, "For what reason are you doing that?" Why questions regularly feel like decisions or accusations as opposed to simple solicitations for information.

7. Listen for emotions by homing in on feeling words. There's one additionally loving question you can ask: "What are you feeling?" That's an invitation for your partner to share emotions: trouble, satisfaction, loneliness, hurt, outrage, disgrace, guilt, love, emptiness, dread, grief, pain, distress, pride, etc. A great

many people feel loved when their partner gives them consolation both to have and communicate feelings. That is the point at which they sense that their partner will go with them into the startling pieces of life.

8.   Let yourself react emotionally to your partner's message. It's essential to listen to your mind. It's considerably increasingly essential to listen with your heart. That implies allowing yourself to sympathize with a portion of your partner's pain and delight. It implies noticing your emotional reactions to your partner's words and feelings. Presently, you would prefer not to get so distracted by your emotional reactions that you quit paying attention to your partner. However, you would like to get at any rate a little emotional.

9.   Read between the lines. Notice what your partner doesn't state just as what the person says. Individuals don't generally say everything they could or precisely what they're thinking. Sometimes they hint. They may decide to utilize delicate words designed not to offend their partner instead of honestly saying what's on their mind. They may share their musings yet not their feelings. Maybe they stop what they're saying, delay, and afterwards switch to another topic. You will notice these things if you ask yourself, "What is my partner leaving out or not quite saying right presently?" Be mindful so as not to make any assumptions, however. Recollect that your partner is the master here, not you. In any case, pointing out hesitations, topic switches, absence of feeling words, or similar omissions might be useful to your partner as the individual in question endeavours to communicate with you.

10.   Save your suggestions until they are mentioned. A few people, especially men, are so anxious to enable their partners to take care of issues that they surge ahead with ideas, suggestions, and plans. The issue is that their partners generally need them to listen as opposed to advising. So, spare your ideas on what to

do until your partner requests them. At that point recollect that your suggestions are only those suggestions. Try not to complain if your partner doesn't tail them.

11.   Be willing to be influenced by your partner's ideas and concerns. John Gottman stresses that great listeners accomplish more than listen to their partner's contemplations, ideas, concerns, and suggestions. They likewise think about those ideas and change what they state or do accordingly. For instance, a lady says to her significant other, "John, you're working excessively hard. I need you to take a break." Notice the difference between responding "Better believe it, no doubt; she generally says that" and "You know, she's right. I'll see about taking next Friday off." Now, individuals don't generally acknowledge their partner's suggestions. The point is to take them seriously regularly and follow up on them in any event occasionally.

Show love by understanding your partner

I am feeling alone. Discrete. Distant. Misunderstood. I am feeling associated with. Close. I am profoundly comprehended. Both of these states are possible in a relationship. Be that as it may, nearly everybody leans towards the last mentioned. Indeed, the primary motivation behind this book is to assist individuals with becoming progressively associated, close, and profoundly comprehended.

This exercise specifically manages to learn how to comprehend your partner all the more likely. That is because taking the time and exertion to comprehend your partner is perhaps the most ideal approaches to show love. Simply think of how magnificent you felt the last time somebody truly comprehended what you were saying the words as well as your feelings, qualities, and dreams. Here's a case of what we're talking about. Tune, a thirty-five-year-old medical secretary, is talking with her better half, Terry, about what's to come. These are her words: "Terry, I'm a little tired of my activity." But this is the thing that she signifies: "Terry, I'm so sick of my activity I could die. I'm exhausted crazy. I can feel myself getting increasingly discouraged each day. I need to quit, yet I'm afraid you'll think I'm irresponsible. Now, Terry isn't a mind peruse. He can't be relied upon consistently to hear what Melody isn't saying. In any case, notice the difference between these possible reactions.

Savvy STRATEGY

Everyone makes some best memories of the day to listen. It might be early morning, late evening, or not long before bedtime. So, if you genuinely need to comprehend your partner better, request that him or her discussion with you at the time you are at your best.

1) A nonresponse: "State, did you realize the Packers are on TV tonight?"

2) A critical reaction: "Well, you can't quit now. We need cash."

3) A quick-solution reaction: "Alright, simply quit your activity if you don't like it."

4) An understanding reaction: "That sounds serious. What's more, you're looking miserable. What's the issue?"

The understanding reaction is different from the others in a few different ways. First, Terry recognizes that Melody just said something important. Second, he notices her emotion. Third, he invites her to state more. It's likely, with that kind of consolation, that Melody will steadily have the option to talk about her considerations, expectations, and fears. She will likewise presumably concoct her solution to this issue. Indeed, she will feel loved. Furthermore, that is our main point. Probably the most ideal ways you can show your partner your love is by taking the time and vitality to get him or her. There is a single word that is highly associated with profound understanding:

1.   "The bridge spanning the abyss that isolates us from one another."

2.   "Active, searching, reaching out toward the other."

3.   "The capacity to comprehend and react to the unique experiences of another."

4.   "Understanding every individual's interest and viewpoint."

5.   "Emotionally understanding the other."

Every one of these definitions says something a little different about compassion—the first hints at why sympathy is such an extraordinary method to show love. Love letters step by step transform into practical little notes: "Nectar, if you don't mind picking up bread and milk in transit home tonight." Our suggestion is sufficiently simple. Set aside the effort to write your partner a love letter at any rate once every month. No, it doesn't need to be ten pages in length. A few will do fine and dandy. A little soft, deepest desires, and your apprehensions and worries as opposed to about your pension, the children's contentions, or your lower back pain.

Most likely, the hardest thing about writing a love letter, if you haven't written one for some time, is getting begun. It might assist you with thinking of writing a love letter like getting prepared to concoct a particularly delicious dish. First, you gather your necessary instruments: pen, paper, and whatnot. At that point, you assemble your centre humour, a great deal of warmth, and, generally significant, your style of sharing the love. Simply recollect as you plan your dish that the objective is to make a feast that both you and your partner find delicious. So, ensure you toss in certain words and contemplations that will be particularly pleasing to your partner. Here's the place we come in. We'll gracefully a portion of the essential ingredients for your letter, in the type of suggestions about what you might need to include. Every ingredient is trailed by a model. Realize, however, that you are the culinary expert responsible for this particular dining experience. Utilize any or the entirety of the ingredients we offer, selecting those that assist you with besting express your love for your partner. Include or take away as you like. Write the letter in your style. Compassion is an approach to get outside of yourself. It helps every one of us meet on that bridge that associates "me" with "you." That prompts the following definition. Every one of us can turn out to be progressively empathic just by actively walking out onto that bridge. We should connect with our partner. As we do that, we will graduate ally figure out how to all the more likely comprehend and react to him or her. It's particularly important, as the creator and psychologist Arthur Carmicle states in the third definition, to realize that your partner has had numerous unique experiences that have moulded his or her life. A portion of these experiences may have been terrible (being explicitly manhandled as a child); others may have been magnificent (having been educated to confide in the universe by a liberal and loving father). Some might be lasting (being a lone child) and others brief (suffering a messed-up collarbone in a traffic accident). Be that as it may, each significant experience has influenced your partner's contemplations, feelings, and worldview. Your partner will feel profoundly comprehended, and loved if you can begin to see the world that the individual in question experiences. The fourth and fifth definitions of sympathy are progressively specific about how compassion functions.

Terry Hargrave, a marriage mentor and writer of a few books on forgiveness, writes that sympathy involves "understanding every individual's interest and viewpoint." He's stressing the need to find out what your partner thinks about essential things in your lives. Another keen creator, John Breech, includes that compassion likewise involves "emotionally under-standing different." His emphasis is on your partner's feelings. Great, you might be thinking about now, that seems like grand theory. However, precisely how might I jump on that bridge? What do I need to do? Indeed, for the most part, what you have to do is relatively simple: pose loads of inquiries and afterwards truly listen without criticism to your partner's answers.

Here's an exercise to help you profoundly comprehend your partner.

Think of two things about your partner's childhood that may have firmly influenced him or her. Make one of them something awful or unfortunate that occurred (losing a parent, parental divorce, moving around a ton, physical maltreatment, and so forth.), the other something great or blessed (having loving grandparents, growing up financially secure, having remarkable holiday traditions, and so forth.). Try not to pick something you've just discussed throughout the years. Instead, select two of your partner's initial experiences that you honestly might want to get familiar with.

Show love by accepting difference

"Indeed, obviously, I love my partner. In any case, if she made two or three little changes, I'd like her more." "He goes through Tuesday nights with his buddies. I wish he'd remain at home with me." "She's more religious than I am. That makes me anxious." Who doesn't need his or her, partner, to change a portion of his or her habits, interests, priorities, friends, or attitudes? Possibly all you need are a couple of changes to a great extent. Maybe you need some significant changes. What about both profound and little changes? Nearly everyone needs to make modifications to his or her partner.

What might occur if you could wave a magic wand and make your partner change in each manner you desire? We speculate that with each change, your partner would turn out to be increasingly more like you. For instance, first, you'd dispose of your partner's affection for reading and substitute watching movies—which is the thing that you like to do most with your extra time. At that point, out would go that drab, quiet method for speaking for a progressively assertive methodology—like yours. At that point, you'd dump that silly love of animals for a progressively realistic attitude, in particular yours. And afterwards... We think that you would inevitably make a clone, your particular twin who acts,

It's the differences between two individuals that make life interesting thinks, and sounds precisely like you. In any case, is that truly what you need from a partner? Shouldn't something be said about the difference? Think about what you gain from the way that your partner has a to some degree different way to deal with life than you do:

Opportunities to attempt new things that you could never at any point think about doing. An opportunity to find out about another method for experiencing the world. Help solving issues from somebody who approaches them differently than you would. Difficulties with your qualities and beliefs that help you decide what is important to you. A little tension that shields your relationship from growing stale.

Probably the ideal approaches to show your love for your partner is to acknowledge for the last time that the person has an option to be different from you. Acknowledgement is the watchword in the above sentence. It assists with breaking it down into three segments: Acceptance implies tolerating, appreciating, and encouraging your partner's differences. Think of these ideas as three stages on a stepping stool that prompts completely accepting your partner. Tolerating your partner's difference is the first step toward full acknowledgement. You endure difference when, even though you don't like what your partner is doing, you don't attempt to prevent him or her from doing it. Resilience is essential in handling every one of those little, annoying things your partner does any other way from you (talks quick, listens to the nation instead of exciting music, skips breakfast, and so forth.). These are "take a full breath and forget about it" issues, only not worth fighting about. Then again, resilience is likewise vital around significant, relationship-threatening differences (for instance, if one individual drink usually and different abhors what liquor does to individuals). These kinds of differences will be negotiated care-completely yet are only here and there settled just by insisting that the other individual acknowledge your qualities and beliefs. The message that goes with resistance is "I can deal with the differences between us without making a tremendous whine."

Love needs trust to frame a solid bond

"I love you. You can confide in me."

It isn't in every case, simple to believe another person. Trust involves vulnerability and being defenceless methods; you could get injured.

Because you love your partner or your partner loves you doesn't necessarily imply that you confide in one another. It's certainly possible to love without trust. Be that as it may, usually relationships dependent on love, those in which trust is missing, are flimsy. They separate easily in lies, omissions, and irresponsibility. Notwithstanding, coupling love with trust is like supergluing two individuals together. The bond made when love is mixed with trust turns out to be practically unbreakable. One difference between love and superglue, however, is that developing trust is a reasonable procedure, made even slower if your partner has been sold out before. That is the reason it's so crucial for you to be consistently reliable. We wrote in the introduction that trying to say "I love you" is insufficient. You should show your love also if you need your partner to feel loved. That idea goes twofold in issues of trust. The individual can be your partner, an old buddy, a parent—any individual who is deserving of your love (i.e., no old lover with whom you are hoping to reunite). Rafael loves Miranda. Be that as it may, he never advises her so. Why? Since he experienced childhood in a family in which men don't communicate any emotion aside from outrage. Indeed, even now, in his thirties, he thinks he'd be giggled at if anyone at any point heard him proclaim his love. Shelby loves Aaron. In any case, she remains quiet about that information.

Individuals have a wide range of explanations behind not saying "I love you." They, for the most part, appear as, "Something terrible will occur if I state that." The unfortunate outcome will originate from their partner, family individuals, or the general community. As it were, they expect some type of punishment for saying "I love you." Now, occasionally they might be right. Sometimes one's partner reacts to "I love you" with the ugliness ("Well, I don't love you") or others do ridicule the speaker ("Oh, Rafael's going delicate"). However, nothing awful would happen a large portion of the times individuals prevent themselves from stating "I love you." Useful things typically follow from saying those words: embraces, smiles, kind words back. So then what truly shields a great many people from saying "I love you"? The appropriate response is old, negative, irrational considerations. For instance, Rafael is convinced that individuals will snicker at him if he says he loves Miranda. In any case, what individuals? What's more, for what reason would that stop him when it's merely both of them at home talking with one another? Furthermore, where did Shelby think of the idea that her saying "I love you" to Aaron gives him power? Quite a while back, a comic book character said, "We have met the adversary, and he is us." That's actually what we're saying here. Shields you from saying "I love you" is you. Cognitive therapists name considerations like Rafael's and Shelby's "irrational." But how about we call them "cold contemplations" here. A virus thought is any idea you have that discourages you from saying something loving, caring, or helpful to your partner. The opposite of cold contemplations is "warm musings." A warm idea is any idea you have that urges you to state something loving, caring, or helpful to your partner. The idea, at that point, is to kick out the cool contemplations from your brain while adding some warm musings. This substitution procedure will help you both state "I love you" all the more frequently and feel good while saying it. You will need to make three basic strides in request to substitute warm musings for cold ones. You can't anticipate that your partner should believe you except if you act dependably.

Am I not catching it means to be reliable? Here are five traits of a trustworthy individual. At the point when you make a promise, try not to be an ignoramus Just to keep it Furthermore, rehash it Does away with Doubting Thomas

1.   He or she says reality, especially in meaningful conversations with his or her partner.

2.   He or she doesn't omit important things from conversations, in any event, while mentioning them might be embarrassing or troubling.

3.   He or she keeps promises, not just big ones (like a pledge to be exporter faithful) yet additionally little everyday understandings.

4.   He or she acts responsibly, reliably, and consistently, demonstrating in daily routines that the person in question can be relied upon.

5.   He or she admits when the individual has messed up and

presents appropriate reparations.

The test is to do every one of the five of these things always. Maybe, being just human, that is asking excessively. We, as a whole, fail the trial of trust-worthiness every so often. To build trust in your relationship, your objective ought to be reliable, not to be for the most part dependable or dependable when it's convenient. One warning: even though being straightforward is an essential piece of building trust, recollect that you can be careful and legit simultaneously. You won't build trust through genuineness if you pair trustworthiness with brutality, awkwardness, roughness, or negligence. How reliable right? Close to every one of the following explanations, place a 0 for "never," a 1 for "sometimes," a 2 for "frequently," a 3 for "more often than not," or a 4 for "consistently."

1.   I come clean with my partner, especially in meaningful conversations.

2.   I don't omit essential things from conversations in any event, when mentioning them might be embarrassing or troubling.

3.   I keep promises, big ones as well as little everyday concernments.

4.   I carry on responsibly, reliably, and consistently, demonstrating in daily routines that my partner can rely upon me.

5.   I admit when I have messed up and present appropriate reparations.

What's your absolute score? Is it in any event 15 points, meaning that you are averaging 3 points an item? If not, you've presumably got a ton of work to do. Where do you most need to change so you can turn out to be more trustworthy? We propose that you pick the one item of these five that would help the most and afterwards begin working on it right away. Recollect one thing as you do as such, however: you don't increase your trustworthiness by making promises. You just become increasingly reliable by keeping them.

Show your love by respecting your partner

Understanding the word regard is critical if two individuals need to have a commonly loving relationship. That is because relationships without regard quickly become monstrous and frightful as each partner makes statements that are particularly damaging to the next. Being in a relationship without regard is like sitting in a paddleboat heading over Niagara Falls. More regrettable yet, it's like being the two individuals sitting in that boat who will not pick up their paddles since they're too bustling shouting insults at one another. So I don't get it means to regard somebody? Maybe the single most assistance definition of regard we've discovered is this one: "to show respect and consideration" (Random House Unabridged Dictionary, Second Edition). In addition to being commonly polite and astute, showing respect and consideration includes listening cautiously to your partner and respecting his or her privacy.

The flip side of regard is called, frequently enough, disrespect. Disrespectful behaviour is typically shaming in that one individual says or implies that there is something amiss with the other. The shame says that the other individual is stupid, terrible, or useless. The shame is an appointed authority which always convicts individuals of being a whole lot of nothing, not adequate, or unlovable. Yet, what precisely does it intend to show respect and consideration to your partner? Here are a quick Dos and Don'ts list.

If You Want to Show Respect to Your Partner, Do

1)   Begin every day with a commitment to approach your partner with deference.

2)   Remember to be as polite to your partner as you would be to a visitor in your home.

3)   Look for and remark on the beneficial things your partner says and does.

4) Let your partner realize that you appreciate his or her basic personality.

5) Listen cautiously and attentively to what your partner says to you.

6)   Support your partner's needs, needs, expectations, and dreams.

7) Tell others what you appreciate about your partner in his or her essence.

8) Regularly acknowledge your partner's choices without trying to transform him or her.

9)   Treat your partner as your equivalent in each manner.

10) Substitute praise for criticism.

11) Laugh at yourself, not at your partner.

12) Affirm your partner's rights to privacy, alone time, and a life of his or her own.

If You Want to Show Respect to Your Partner, Don't

1) Always criticize your partner.

2) Swear at your partner.

3) Say or imply that your partner is terrible, evil, stupid, useless, incompetent, or appalling.

4) Say dreadful things to your partner before others.

5) Ignore what your partner is saying or go about as though the person isn't there.

6) Act superior to your partner.

7) Tell your partner that the individual in question is unlovable.

8) Act disgusted or incredibly disappointed with your partner.

9) Find things amiss with how your partner says and gets things done.

10) Tell your partner that the person in question is not in the same class as another person (make an unfavourable comparison).

11) Hit, push, push, or physically compromise your partner.

12) Regularly take steps to kick your partner out of your life and find somebody better.

13) Try to control everything your partner does (to run such an individual's reality).

14) Refuse to state "I love you" since you are furious with him or her.

It will be ideal if you take a decent, long gander at these two lists. Circle the items on the Dos list that you most need to recall. Accomplish all the more frequently. They will increase your regard for your partner. At that point circle the items on the Don'ts list that you most need to chip away at. These are the things you have been doing that decline the measure of regard you show your partner. The following stage is to decide which a couple of items on each list you will concentrate on changing. Select close to two items from each list, so you aren't overpowered. At that point, take the following week to practice them. For the test, if you select "Don't find things amiss with how your partner says and gets things done" and "Do make sure to be as polite to your partner as you would be to a visitor in your home," think about those two items consistently. Ensure you refrain from excessive negativity and simultaneously make sure to request things politely and to state thank you in any event, for little demonstrations of kindness your partner shows you. Be a little intense on yourself here. Begin thanking your partner for those kind words and acts. Try not to try too hard. A simple "thank you" is typically enough to tell your partner you've noticed what the individual has recently done. The most effective method to avoid the slide into defensiveness (just looking for the terrible stuff) We've mentioned before that we are marriage mentors. Tragically, it's frequently during couples' sessions that we get exercises on what turns out badly in relationships. We call one truly predictable example, the "slide into defensiveness." This slide happens when pained and anxious individuals begin watching just for their partner's criticisms, negative remarks, or different assaults. They are so worried about defending against the following assault that they remain on steady caution. They carry on like soldiers guarding the perimeter of their territory, ignoring anything that isn't threatening with the goal that their entire vitality can concentrate on survival. Sometimes these frightened soldiers even begin firing at shadows, convinced that the adversary must be out there. In any case, your partner isn't a foe soldier. * He or she isn't loading a weapon right now as you read this book. Your partner might be heading your way with a cold glass of lemonade or some tea intended only for you. Practice taking in love each time you give it out: Breathe in silver and inhale out gold A few peruses of this exercise manual may find it easier to give love than to receive it. Others might be only the opposite, happier with taking in love than giving it out. In any case, the vast majority feel best when they achieve harmony between these two reciprocal parts of human compassion. In this exercise, we describe a Buddhist way to deal with helping individuals discover and maintain balance in life. This exercise is particularly helpful as to balancing taking in and giving out love.

The Buddhists know and comprehend a great deal about breath and how breathing brings spirit into (inspires) the body, just as how breath and body fit into the universe. One school of Buddhist idea depends on compassion. There is a particular breathing exercise; this gathering of Buddhists likes to do. This exercise is not painful, and as we ace it, we quiet our spirit while increasing. Try not to rationalize demonstrations of disrespect or for failing to show regard when you could have. Your objective ought to be to demonstrate regard to your partner the entire day.

One important note: kindly don't transform these lists into a "See, nectar, this is the thing that you are doing incorrectly" address. That is not aware. Instead, maintain the emphasis on what you have to do in request to exhibit that you regard your partner. Roll out the improvements you have to make. Continue making them. The odds are genuinely acceptable that if you do, your partner will get the idea and treat you all the more deferentially, as well.

CHAPTER 3

Difference between making Sex and Love

Your utilization of language may differ from our own. Be that as it may, for us, "having sex" signifies the physical demonstration of intercourse. "Making love" includes having sex yet includes the verbal, emotional, and spiritual connections that happen during sexual union. Of the two experiences, just making love makes genuine intimacy. As brilliant all things considered to engage in sexual relations with one another, making love is surprisingly better. We defined intimacy before as "two individuals sharing their private universes and profoundly respecting each other's disclosures." We included that a couple achieves intimacy when everyone faces the challenge of sharing mysteries, and both react with loving, caring, interest, and acknowledgement. Intimacy begins when one individual decides, "I'll take a risk by telling you something important about myself", and the different reacts, "Proceed. We're in this together. You can believe me with whatever you let me know. What's more, I'll inform you concerning myself, as well."

There is nothing about having sex that automatically makes it over an approach to achieve real joy. Two individuals can remain hidden from one another even while they deal with their requirements. They can even become sexual competitors, having sex with extraordinary skill; however, no emotion, the equivalent of excessively practised formal dancers who impeccable each progression while looking at one another with solidified smiles. These sexual competitors regularly appear to be willing to sacrifice the emotional connection in their mission for the perfect climax.

Presently, there's nothing amiss with straightforward as can be a delight. We're not suggesting that each time several hits the sack, they should achieve the heights of intimacy. Sometimes—ordinarily—the objective of having sex is physical discharge. In any case, not generally. Sometimes individuals need more than that. They need to feel profoundly associated physically as well as emotion-partner and spiritually. They need this particular demonstration of intercourse to turn into an intimate experience. Love letters step by step transform into practical little notes: "Nectar, if you don't mind picking up bread and milk in transit home tonight." Our suggestion is sufficiently simple. Set aside the effort to write your partner a love letter at any rate once every month. No, it doesn't need to be ten pages in length. A few will do fine and dandy. A little soft, deepest desires, and your apprehensions and worries as opposed to about your pension, the children's contentions, or your lower back pain. Most likely, the hardest thing about writing a love letter, if you haven't written one for some time, is getting begun. It might assist you with thinking of writing a love letter like getting prepared to concoct a particularly delicious dish. First, you gather your necessary instruments: pen, paper, and whatnot. At that point, you assemble your centre humour, a great deal of warmth, and, generally significant, your style of sharing the love. Simply recollect as you plan your dish that the objective is to make a feast that both you and your partner find delicious. So, ensure you toss in certain words and contemplations that will be particularly pleasing to your partner. Here's the place we come in. We'll gracefully a portion of the essential ingredients for your letter, in the type of suggestions about what you might need to include. Every ingredient is trailed by a model. Realize, however, that you are the culinary expert responsible for this particular dining experience. Utilize any or the entirety of the ingredients we offer, selecting those that assist you with besting express your love for your partner. Include or take away as you like. Write the letter in your style. Furthermore, what preferable spot over the room could there be to discover genuine intimacy? Sex is by its very nature an intensely private occasion. We close the entryway. We talk in whispers. We state and do things that we would not need individuals to watch or catch. We let ourselves be vulnerable to one another. We let go of control. What an opportunity to experience each part of the shared connection.

There is no single equation to transform having sex into making love. Each couple does that in a particular manner. Be that as it may, we can offer some suggestions that might assist you with moving in that direction.

1) Don't surge. Hurried sex is never intimate sex. While you're grinding away, and a while later.

2) Seduce your partner's heart just as his or her body. State and do what you've realized indeed cause your partner to feel loved during intercourse. If you don't have the foggiest idea, inquire.

3) Take a few risks. Offer a dream. Take a stab at something different. Risk feeling silly or foolish. Risk rejection for possible acknowledgement.

4) Encourage your partner to mention to you what the individual truly needs. It's alright to disapprove of those desires, obviously, yet consider saying yes in the spirit of shared experience.

5) Think of sexuality as grown-up playtime. Have a great time. Chuckle. Appreciate.

6) Take incredible bliss in helping your partner feel brilliant. Delicately invite your partner to forsake control.

7) Accept what is advertised. Start with the idea that your partner owes you nothing in the region of sexuality. Graciously acknowledge what you receive without expecting or demanding more.

8) Remember to state much obliged.

9) Relax. Try not to leave any opportunity for intimacy alone spoiled by focusing on execution. In particular, don't worry about getting to climax or getting your partner there. You'll arrive when you arrive. What's more, sometimes, the sexual union can be satisfying without climax.

10) Show appreciation for and refrain from criticizing your partner (or yourself) previously, during, or after intercourse. The kind of intimacy we're discussing just happens in a climate of trust, security, and acknowledgement. In particular, offer just positive remarks about your partner's body.

11) Focus your mind on the present. Intimacy happens when your mind is centred around the occasion. Spot your distractions on a psychological rack while you have intercourse. They'll be there ASAP waiting for you when you're set. We propose you read this list throughout whenever you begin thinking about making love. Select a couple of ideas from the list that you will recall. Use them.

Perhaps the best time to show your love is during a conflict

"Nectar, I don't concur with you by any stretch of the imagination. I think you're off-base and I'm right. Be that as it may, I still love you a ton." Perhaps the best time to show that you love your partner is during a conflict. Why? Since the vast majority fall away from secure connection during fights with their partners and become progressively dreadful, preoccupied, or dis-missive. They may look and sound furious, yet they likely feel insecure, highly emotional, and disconnected. It's downright painful to feel loved during a contention. So that is actually when individuals most need to get some consolation. They have to hear right without even a moment's pause that they are loved. Telling your partner about your love consoles him or her that your love is sufficiently able to climate any disagreement, anyway serious or durable. It is probably the most grounded explanation of faith you can make. So, the first thing to recall is to state "I love you" to your partner in any event, during the conflict. In any case, there are different approaches to show your partner your love during a disagreement. There are likewise some unloving things you will need to avoid doing. How about we begin with those by reviewing a portion of crafted by John Gottman. Work has inquired about couples for quite a long time. He will probably have the option to predict which couples will in the end divorce and which will remain married. It's anything but difficult to get frantic, even contemptuous, during a contention. That is when individuals direct terrible sentiments toward one another. Afterwards, they may apologize and state they didn't mean it that way. Be that as it may, it's past the point of no return by at that point. So, make sure to state "I love you" when you disagree. That way, you won't need to feel terrible later.

Four of them are being excessively critical of one's partner, expressing disdain, being excessively defensive, and "stonewalling" (refusing to discuss issues). These are negative behaviours that certainly should be avoided in any profoundly loving relationship. It's particularly important to avoid them during conflicts. Simply think about how any of those behaviours nearly ensures that a little conflict will quickly grow into a significant dispute. Criticism, scorn, defensiveness, and stonewalling make distance and diminish love.

Dr Gottman recorded that, presumably to no one's surprise, pretty much every couple disagrees, contends, and fights. No two individuals can concur about everything throughout the years. Some conflict is ordinary. Hide thermoses, the sheer measure of conflict did not predict divorce. Some stable couples disagreed a ton, others infrequently. What did matter, however, was how they contended. Gottman discovered that what truly helped was the point at which the ladies in long haul relationships "mollified" the beginning of a possible conflict discussion ("Honey, I truly appreciate your feeding the child. However, she should get bananas, not ground hurl" versus "How might you feed the infant ground throw! Think carefully!") and when men responded less defensively ("Okay, I'll listen to what she's saying" versus "How could you criticize me!") and let their partners influence their considerations and actions ("Hmm, perhaps she has a point there" versus "She's an idiot. I'm right and that is all there's to it"). Gottman's findings appear to pressure the requirement for couples to be civil during disagreements. This is your partner, all things considered, not the foe. Here's a list of some different things, in addition to "I love you," that you can say and do during a conflict that will enable your partner to feel loved.

1) Offer to get your partner a soda pop, some espresso, or a tidbit.

2) Give or acknowledge an embrace (however just if your partner concurs; ask first).

3) Say positive things about your partner's ideas instead of criticizing ("You know, what you just said makes sense even though I still can't concur with your main point").

4) Stay quiet: inhale profoundly, talk gradually, sit down, keep your voice delicate.

5) Fight fair: be polite, remain on topic, don't swear, don't assault your partner's personality.

6) Look for commonly pleasing solutions to your disagreements. Be happy to negotiate and compromise.

7) Be deferential: avoid shaming, humiliating, and blaming articulations. These are not approaching to show your love. They under-mine love each time you use them. If you do say something impolite or negligent, apologize immediately and don't do it again.

8) Be forgiving and accepting. Your partner can't state and do everything precisely how you'd like, especially during a disagreement. So don't think about things too literally. Try not to get oversensitive. Cut your partner a little leeway, and with any karma, the person in question will do likewise for you.

Blessings the individual genuinely needs

It's five-year-old Joey's birthday festivity, in conclusion, he gets the chance to open up that gigantic present he's been looking at for the last week. Joey vigorously tears open the group—and a while later starts crying wildly. What was the arrangement? Taking everything into account, Joey had convinced himself that the group contained a bicycle and instead it held a PC structured distinctly for youngsters. Joey's people feel out and out terrible now. They were sure he would cherish that PC (regardless of the way that Joey had mentioned the bicycle on a couple of events and never referenced a PC). Father was especially disappointed considering the way that he cherishes PCs himself and wouldn't perceive any issues whatsoever accepting one as a present on his birthday. By and by he's getting angry with his youngster disliking the blessing and at himself for settling on an ill-advised decision. In the interim, Mom is thinking about whether they ought to re-establish the PC or demand that Joey make sense of how to use it.

There's a little Joey inside us all concerning feel adored. That is the bit of us that knows correctly what we need from others. Exactly when we get the real blessing, we feel great. In any case, we feel awful when we are offered an improper blessing. In reality, the Joey inside all of us may even feel disliked when we get an improper blessing, thinking something like, "Sure, it's pleasant that she values my looks, anyway what I need most is to be acknowledged for how I think. I wish just once she'd state I offered a savvy remark."

Splendid TIP

Bring a stone home or take him rock picking. On the off chance that your accomplice likes catastrophe books, discover them for her. In particular, if your accomplice feels adored when you're there, take a brief reprieve to be there. The issue here isn't this adult Joey's accomplice is primary. No, she's genuinely attempting to state something pleasant. She needs him to feel much improved. It's not her imperfection, yet she's submitted a comparable mistake that little Joey's people made. She's given him a wrong blessing, and now the two feel hopeless and neglected.

There must be a thousand distinct ways you could show your affection to your partner. In any case, which of those thousand prospects would make your accomplice feel commonly cherished? In what capacity may you tell? It would be unimaginable if your accomplice reliably let you know decisively what the person being referred to required. Yet, you can't rely upon that to occur as a general rule (obviously the adult Joey in the model above hasn't yet instructed his accomplice concerning his ought to be commended for his thoughts).

Nevertheless, indeed, the principal strategy to address your accomplice's issues and needs are to listen care-totally when the person being referred to communicates their wants or speaks with everything taken into account about what makes the person in question feel incredible. Another way is to see whatever makes your accomplice's eyes light up with charm. A third way, ordinarily, is to ask your accomplice what you can say or do that genuinely feels adoring. That is the point of convergence of our next exercise. Note that we're merely going to get some data about what you may do here, not what you may state, yet a comparable standard applies in each district.

Achieve something liberal for your accomplice

Love to your accomplice is by being liberal. That suggests going somewhat out of your way to deal with achieve something decent for the person in question, something that you don't have to do and isn't healthy or mentioned. Showings of liberality are now and again seemingly insignificant details like bringing your accomplice a cut of pizza from that bistro the individual loves or doing the dishes despite the way that it's not your turn. Nonetheless, now and again shows of liberality are far higher than that: purchasing a plane ticket so she can visit her pregnant young lady in Germany, tolerating the lost canine he has started to look all naive at, consenting to move to an enormous house notwithstanding the way that you are content with the one you have. Am I not finding its importance to be liberal? Word reference definitions incorporate "unselfish," "liberal in giving or sharing," "freed from disagreeableness or littleness of the psyche," "providing for others something of huge worth," "being warm and thoughtful to others," and "a status to give."

Interestingly, two of the antonyms of liberality are "miserliness" and "unimportance." These words signal a specific smallness of character, a holding tight to whatever one has. Liberality is the particular inverse of that sort of modesty. The liberal individual offers their wealth and improves as a person because of it. Make an effort not to consider liberality a penance. The liberal individual needs to provide for others. It feels good, not terrible. One more thing: the extremely liberal individual doesn't provide for another with a desire for getting something back. An incredibly liberal blessing reliably goes with no curveballs. The message is, "Here, take this. I need you to have it. I don't require or foresee anything like this. You don't owe me anything. It just fulfils me to have the choice to offer this to you." Maybe you starting at now consider yourself a reasonably liberal person.

Unanticipated amazements add feeling to your relationship

It's not a dozen roses on their birthday that checks the most. It's the single rose you get in travel home one night for no good reason in any way shape or form. Moreover, the little note on the pad saying "I love you." And the proposition to take the children to the zoo so your accomplice can have some necessary alone time this week's end. Additionally, the sensitive hold onto you give as the individual being referred to is cruising by. Also, all of those other small, frightening shows of benevolence, sagacity, and generosity that unexpected your accomplice. These are the blessings that tell your accomplice that you are consistently pondering the person in question. They also pass on the message that you genuinely need your accomplice to feel adored and thought reliably. Think about these little indications of thought as the what tops off an already good thing of adoration. They help the whole cake taste better and look better. There's one more clarification, nonetheless, to give alarming astonishments to your accomplice. Perhaps this is the best clarification of every: alarming astonishment help keep the opinion in your relationship.

Insightful HUMOR

A kiss on the catch A pinch on the ear A warm sweater A gesture of congratulations A thing that is pretty much nothing or out of schedule an energetic jest A nectarine A sensitive back rub Upon your shoulder Makes you warm Instead of colder way continually. Regardless, routinely connections become horrendously viable and sensible after some time. Very to get directly to the point, connections get stale when they become unnecessarily unsurprising. In any case, it's frequently hard to make space for long sentimental intermissions, for instance, seven days off in the Bahamas. That is the spot these unexpected amazements come in. They help keep the assumption in your relationship reliably, making the relationship both less unsurprising but instead progressively pleasant. So, what's the formula for this sentimental good to beat all of the adoration? Endeavour this blend.

1) Spontaneity—doing pleasant things unexpectedly without a considerable amount of arranging.

2) Thoughtfulness—knowing the seemingly insignificant details that your accomplice genuinely increases in value.

3) Playfulness—astounding your join forces with stuff that gets a laugh.

4) Adventurousness—being eager to have a go at something

whether or not you don't have a clue how much your accomplice will value it.

5)   Unpredictability—breaking the shape by giving a blessing or accomplishing something for your accomplice you've never done.

Marty is acceptable at saying "I love you" to his partner, Freddy. Indeed, the ace claims his love a few times every day. The issue is that he frequently utilizes that state as a feature of a reason, as in "I'm heartbroken, Freddy. I neglected to pick up the groceries. Be that as it may, I love you." He likewise utilizes "I love you" to get what he needs: "Freddy, I love you to such an extent. State, you wouldn't occur to have a couple of additional dollars on you, OK? I need gas cash." Georgianna must state "I love you" a hundred times per day. "I love you, pass the spread." "I love you, the nice climate we're having, isn't it?". " Her family not, at this point, even hears those words. They've lost their emotional impact.

"I love you" is presumably the most critical explanation anybody can make. Those words are incredible, compelling, compassionate, and exciting. Indeed, the vast majority of the exercises in this book are intended to assist individuals with saying them all the more frequently. In any case, "I love you" can be misused (like by Marty) or abused (like by Georgianna). Remember these guidelines. Do state "I love you" much of the time. Recall that this expression is a full miracle gift you can give your partner. Nothing is gained by not saying "I love you" when you feel love. So don't be stingy with your words.

1)   Mean it when you state it. Presently, you might resent or discontent with your partner and still say "I love you" to him or her. You don't need to be glad to feel loving. However, it is essential that you feel, if just for an instant, the unique sensations that accompany truly loving somebody. Make

sure to set aside a little effort to feel reality in your words as you state them.

2) Keep your actions consistent with the idea of love. Make sure to coordinate your words with your deeds. Loving actions are the ideal complement to loving words.

3) Don't state "I love you" just out of habit.

4) Don't state "I love you" to get something you need. Do that all the time, and you'll before long hear this reaction: "Gracious, sure you love me. So what do you need this time?"

5) Don't pair the expression "I love you" with criticism or negativity. Saying things like "It's simply because I love you that I'm telling you that you have to get more fit [get work, quit drinking]" contaminates the expression.

We just mentioned six issues regarding the underuse, abuse, and misuse of the expression "I love you." Select the issue that most debilitates your relationship—the one that most shields your partner from feeling profoundly loved. At that point, make an individual commitment to change that behaviour.

6) If the issue is that you neglect to state "I love you" when you could, at that point you have to commit to state "I love you" all the more frequently. There are a few exercises in this book can assist you with doing that.

7) If the issue is that you state "I love you" however don't set aside the effort to feel it, at that point you have to back off,

inhale, and a sense that emotion. You have to concentrate on quality more than quantity here, feeling the impact of every "I love you" on your body, mind, and soul.

If the issue is that you state "I love you" however go about as though you don't, at that point you have to begin treating your partner with more prominent regard, caring, consideration, and keenness. Otherwise, all you are giving is the illusion of love wrapping paper without anything genuine inside. If the issue is that you state "I love you" to get something you need, at that point you should quit running that particular con game. Quit trying to manipulate your partner. Love is tied in with caring for your partner, not using him or her. It might be difficult to stop this behaviour, primarily if it's worked before. Ultimately, however, it will merit the exertion if you need to experience the feeling of genuine love. Practice saying "I love you" without asking for, wanting, or expecting anything. If the issue is that you state "I love you" only out of habit, at that point give cutting a shot that expresses totally for a couple of days. Notice all the times you ordinarily would state "I love you" automatically, without genuine feeling, yet don't state it. At that point, after you have abstained for some time, begin saying "I love you," yet ration yourself at first to close to twice per day to any single individual. Set aside the effort to feel your love each time you state it. If the issue is that you state "I love you" however pair that expresses with negativity or criticism, at that point never under any circumstance follow that sentence with "yet" (as in, "I love you, yet you did that all off-base") or some other type of criticism. If you do want to be critical or negative (everyone does now and again. However, we trust you don't try too hard), at that point simply feel free to state what you need to state without any reference to love.

Recognize the estimation of both closeness and impermanent separation

Love, for individual couples, feels like a three-step dance played by a string group of four. For other people, it's a hard rock show featuring electric guitars, a square move total with fiddlers, or a deep song. Frequently reminds us of a loving partnership is an accordion. Why? Due to the way the roars of the accordion, first filling up with air in request to have the option to cause notes and afterwards contracting as the sounds to rise, takes after the way that loving couples handle their requirements for closeness and short separation in their relationship. One of the territories in a partnership that each couple must negotiate is distancing. Questions like the ones underneath must be asked and replied, typically once as well as many times over the length of the relationship.

1) Do we need to fraternize today?
2) Is it alright to need to escape from one another for a little time?

The vast majority have times when they need to get genuinely near their partner. These are the times when they desire to share meaningful conversation, have intercourse, walk side by side. The message they pass on to their partner at these minutes is "I'm happy we're as one." However, these equivalent individuals additionally will feel a desire to invest some energy separated from their partner. That is the point at which they need to be separated from everyone else or with others. The message they pass on to their partner at these times is "Right now I need some distance." Meanwhile, their partners have similar requirements for closeness and distance. So, at any one time, there are four distinct possibilities:

1. I need closeness, and you need closeness.

2.   I need distance, and you need distance.

3.   I need closeness, and you need distance.

4.   I need distance, and you need closeness.

Presently, the first two situations are anything but difficult to manage. The accordion makes extraordinary music without a note of disharmony. You and your partner easily associate for some time or invest some energy away from one another by shared permission. Those two options might follow one another. Imagine, for instance, a couple that makes intense love and afterwards happily drifts off into isolated rooms to peruse, write, or work separated.

One of you needs closeness and the other distance. What's going to occur? Will one of you wind up feeling covered because the different insists on an excessive amount of harmony? Will one of you feel isolated and desolate because different won't draw near? In what manner can one accordion play good music when two individuals are taking a starting to get it to do different things? There are two keys to dealing with this issue: individual mindfulness and shared discussion/negotiation.

Common Discussion/Negotiation

Here are five ideas that will assist you in discussing and negotiate distancing issues with your partner.

1.   Both closeness and separation are ordinary and vital in any stable relationship.

2.   It's alright to support your requirements for closeness and

distance. It's alright for your partner to shout out too. Common differences that must be acknowledged.

3.   Getting close doesn't mean you'll get covered. You can make distance when you need it.

4.   Taking time separated doesn't mean the relationship is awful or frail. Have faith that both of you will need to reconnect in the wake of spending time away from one another.

5.   You will have the option to address both of your issues for closeness and separation more often than not if you continue talking.

Along these lines, if you are doing this exercise with your partner, if you don't want mindset aside the effort to recite what you just worked so anyone can hear to your partner. Listen cautiously to your partner's announcement, as well. Discuss how you can give each other clear signals when you need time together or separated—discussion about any feelings of trepidation either of you might have about getting excessively close or excessively distant. Check whether you can recall times when one of you needed closeness and the different distance. How could you handle those situations? How might you handle them better later on?

If you are doing this exercise alone, think about how you have taken care of your requirement for closeness and separation in past and current relationships. Likewise, think about how you've managed your partners' requirements for closeness and separation. At that point, think about how you can utilize this knowledge to upgrade your present or future relationships.

There must be fifty different ways to love a leaver: Helping the partner who runs from closeness in pretty much every relationship one individual is a little happier with showing affection than the other. That is typical. However, in particular relationships, the difference is immense. One partner is brimming with love and needs to show it a great deal. Meanwhile, the other partner keeps down, shying endlessly both from giving and receiving messages of love. That individual goes about as though the person were brought into the world with internal love diverters designed to keep out intimacy. What's more, if those redirectors don't function admirably enough, sometimes that individual only level out flees from love, fleeing to the television set, the carport, or the shopping community. As far as grown-up connection style this partner is generally either Dismissive ("I am independent—I needn't bother with anyone's love") or Fearful ("I'm terrified to take in love—I feel too helpless when I do"). A considerable lot of the exercises in this book are designed to help these love deflectors figure out how to communicate and receive love messages. Be that as it may, not this one. We've written this exercise for those of you who are baffled because your partner is a love redirector. You attempt to tell your partner the amount you love him or her. Shockingly, your partner appears not to notice your endeavours, fails to react lovingly, flees, or even angrily dismisses your love offerings. At those times you might discover yourself thinking something like, "For what reason do I trouble trying to show my partner, my love, when all I get back is a shrug? What's the utilization?" Remember, however, your partner probably truly needs to feel your love. It's merely that the individual isn't excellent at it. Possibly your partner experienced childhood in an unloving or undemonstrative home. Maybe your partner is firearm bashful because the individual in question endured numerous rejections or disloyalties previously. Whatever the explanation, you're in this relationship together, so you might also continue trying to communicate your love. A portion of your love will undoubtedly get past those redirectors. At that point, your partner will realize that being loved is a great feeling. Here's a simple recipe to follow with your love-bashful partner:

Be acknowledge of your partner's limitations. Show restraint. Be creative.

1) Be accepting of your partner's limitations. Your partner is frightened of intimacy. That is a reality. So, if you push excessively hard, excessively quick, or excessively long, your partner will be overpowered. That is the point at which the person will set up the redirector or flee. You'll be delicate in your approach and be happy to step back if a particular idea doesn't work. Most importantly, don't request, address, guilt-trip, or ask for love.

2) Be patient. Have faith that the quality of your love will bite by bit over-come your partner's feelings of trepidation. This will require significant investment, however. Not days but instead, months and years. Be that as it may, individuals do change, and partners who are afraid of intimacy can figure out how to take in love at more profound and more profound levels. Search for signs of progress after some time, for example, your partner slowly going from saying, "Uh-huh" when you state "I love you" to responding with, "I love you, as well" to saying "I love you" first.

3) Be creative. That is the place the title of this exercise comes in (with a little assistance from the songwriter Paul Simon). The idea is to search for simple approaches to show your love that doesn't automatically trigger your partner's love redirector.

There must be fifty different ways to love a leaver

1. Fold a "Coincidentally, and I love you" note into your partner's handbag, schoolbag, or briefcase.

2. Give your partner a startling little gift, for example, a mug with his or her name on it.

3. Contact your partner delicately on the arm to pass on your love.

4. Non Verbal Loving Feeling.

5. Propose going to a movie that you know is special for your partner.

6. Hangover and whisper "I love you" without expecting a re-action.

7. Play "your" tune on the CD player.

8. Make your partner's favourited feast.

9. Help your partner with work that the person regularly does alone.

10. Bring your partner some espresso when the individual is fascinated in an errand.

11. Tell your partner that the person is unique.

12. Praise your partner when the person communicates love to

you or the kids.

13. Peruse the paper beside your partner instead of in the other room.

14. State, "It's alright when you don't answer me when I state 'I love you.' I still love you."

15. Rehash your love messages if your partner doesn't appear to hear you the first time.

16. Ask your partner what the person is thinking about when the individual is quiet.

17. Step up to the plate and make times when you two can be as one.

18. Sit close to your partner and do your own thing.

19. Whisper "romantic things" in your partner's ear.

20. State "I love you" energetically instead of seriously.

21. Ask your partner what is unnerving about being in love and simply listen.

22. Put a cover around your partner on a cold day.

23. Go to a place of worship together and afterwards talk about the message.

24. Write a sonnet about your love for your partner.

25. Get some information about what the person in question truly needs in life.

26. Ask your partner what love intends to him or her.

27. Ask your partner what you do that encourages him, or her vibe loved.

28. Tell your partner when something the individual in question does cause you to feel loved.

29. Reach over and hold your partner's hand on a walk.

30. Clasp turns in public if that isn't unreasonably embarrassing for your partner.

31. Promise your partner that you are sticking near.

32. Thank your partner only for being a decent individual.

33. Require a few minutes in the middle of your bustling day.

34. Offer a decent joke together so you can hear each other's chuckling.

35. Release your partner away without making him or her vibe guilty.

36. Kiss your partner on the highest point of the head.

37. Toss in an "I love you" when it's least anticipated.

38. Send roses.

39. Ask your partner how love was communicated in his or her family.

40. Notice and mention how your partner gives you love without saying "I love you."

41. In your partner's quality, explain to others how and why you love your partner.

42. Deromanticize your love life by making an extraordinary exertion to tempt your partner.

43. Tell your partner you can feel his or her love for you and that it feels better.

44. Remind your partner that the individual in question is loved "just on the off chance that you overlooked."

45. Give your partner a quick embrace.

46. Delicately urge your partner to feel free to say "I love you" all the more regularly.

47. Console your insecure partner that the individual in question is loved and adorable.

48. Make a mystery "I love you" message that you can share without others knowing.

49. Set aside some effort to show appreciation when your partner says "I love you."

50. Request that your partner turn off his or her love diverters for a couple of moments.

Ladies (and we think a few men, as well) are biologically customized to react to an infant's needs.

Bit by bit, infants react to the parent answering their cry by quitting crying as well as with a smile. They recognize their folks' countenances. Particular security builds up that transforms "I'm any infant being dealt with by any mother" into "I'm a unique child being dealt with by my unparalleled one mom." That's the way "Feed me" develops into "Love me." From a child's point of view, at that point, you can't separate being loved from being sustained. To a child, it's typical, familiar, and essential to take in another's love.

Each partner the two gives and receives nurturance from the other. (Not generally in equivalent sums, however. One regular complaint we hear in marriage counselling is that one individual thinks the person gives far more than 50 per cent to the next. As a rule, in American society, it is the lady who feels overburdened and under nurtured.) Also, grown-ups have a full scope of needs and needs. It's not, at this point simply "Feed me" yet "Feed me and hold me and have intercourse to me and invest energy with me and talk with me and listen to me and disclose to me you love me." Our main point, however, is nearly equivalent to previously: similarly, likewise, with children, it's natural, ordinary, and essential for grown-ups to take in their partner's love.

Someplace along the way of life, be that as it may, a few people may have put some distance between this simple truth. If that has transpired, at that point, you avoid taking in nurturing and love. In particular, you regularly ignore decline or reject your partner's endeavours to deal with you. Maybe you experienced childhood in a home where you didn't watch a lot of love-giving or love-taking, so it doesn't appear to be right to need that now. Or then again, perhaps you were informed that individuals should just give and never receive. Whatever the reasons, today you realize that you don't take in a ton of the love that your partner offers you. Consciously or unconsciously, you usually deliver a "No, much appreciated, dear" message to your partner. "No, much obliged; I don't need your veiling. No, much obliged; I needn't bother with your delicacy. No, much obliged; I won't take your solace. No, much appreciated; I can't take your love." It will be ideal if you take a decent, long gander at these two lists. Circle the items on the Dos list that you most need to recall. Accomplish all the more frequently. They will increase your regard for your partner. At that point circle the items on the Don'ts list that you most need to chip away at. These are the things you have been doing that decline the measure of regard you show your partner. The following stage is to decide which a couple of items on each list you will concentrate on changing. Select close to two items from each list, so you aren't overpowered. At that point, take the following week to practice them. For the test, if you select "Don't find things amiss with how your partner says and gets things done" and "Do make sure to be as polite to your partner as you would be to a visitor in your home," think about those two items consistently. Ensure you refrain from excessive negativity and simultaneously make sure to request things politely and to state thank you in any event, for little demonstrations of kindness your partner shows you. Be a little intense on yourself here. Begin thanking your partner for those kind words and acts. Try not to try too hard. A simple "thank you" is typically enough to tell your partner you've noticed what the individual has recently done. The most effective method to avoid the slide into defensiveness (just looking for the terrible stuff) We've mentioned before that we are marriage mentors. Tragically, it's frequently during couples' sessions that we get exercises on what turns out badly in relationships. We call one truly predictable example, the "slide into defensiveness." This slide happens when pained and anxious individuals begin watching just for their partner's criticisms, negative remarks, or different assaults. They are so worried about defending against the following assault that they remain on steady caution. They carry on like soldiers guarding the perimeter of their territory, ignoring anything that isn't threatening with the goal that their entire vitality can concentrate on survival. Sometimes these frightened soldiers even begin firing at shadows, convinced that the adversary must be out there. In any case, your partner isn't a foe soldier. * He or she isn't loading a weapon right now as you read this book. Your partner might be heading your way with a cool glass of lemonade or some tea intended only for you. Practice taking in love each time you give it out: Breathe in silver and inhale out gold A few peruses of this exercise manual may find it easier to give love than to receive it. Others might be only the opposite, happier with taking in love than giving it out. In any case, the vast majority feel best when they achieve harmony between these two reciprocal parts of human compassion. In this exercise, we describe a Buddhist way to deal with helping individuals discover and maintain balance in life. This exercise is particularly helpful as to balancing taking in and giving out love. The Buddhists know and comprehend a great deal about breath and how breathing brings spirit into (inspires) the body, just as how breath and body fit into the universe. One school of Buddhist idea depends on compassion. There is a particular breathing exercise. This gathering of Buddhists likes to do. This exercise is not difficult, and as we ace it, we quiet our spirit while increasing. Try not to rationalize demonstrations of disrespect or for failing to show regard when you could have. Your objective ought to be to demonstrate regard to your partner the entire day. One important note: kindly don't transform these lists into a "See, nectar, this is the thing that you are doing incorrectly" address. That is not aware. Instead, maintain the emphasis on what you have to do in request to exhibit that you regard your partner. Roll out the improvements you have to make. Continue making them. The odds are truly acceptable that if you do, your partner will get the idea and treat you all the more deferentially, as well.

We have different exercises in this section designed to assist you with figuring out how and why you guard against taking love. Those exercises will assist you with understanding and challenge the wellsprings of your discomfort about making love in. In any case, here we aren't as interested in those things. Instead, we trust you permit yourself to take in your partner's love. We believe that nearly anybody reading this book can make an understood, conscious choice to take in their partner's love. It's basically up to you. No one can make you take in love, caring, and kindness. You can square it for eternity.

There's hardly any writing involved with this exercise. You should simply sign your name to the promise proposed beneath. Nonetheless, we ask that you not merely quickly sign and run off to the following exercise. If you don't want mindset aside the effort to think your promise through, ask yourself these inquiries: What might it truly mean to me if I let myself completely take in my partner's love? By what means might do so influence me? By what method might it impact my partner? Am I truly prepared to make this promise to myself? Would I be able to bring it through? Am I signing since I think I ought to or because I need to? Is this my free choice that doesn't feel like an obligation, sacrifice, or weight?

Put your "no" on the rack: Choosing to allow in your partner's love

You are indeed blessed if you have someone in your life who reveals to you that the individual loves you and does loving things for you. Be that as it may, those demonstrations of kindness and caring are just bravoed if you can take them in. If you have created habits that shield you from accepting those words and demonstrations of love, at that point, they are squandered. Individuals avoid love—Scratch off the ones that you do most much of the time.

Fail to notice the beautiful things their partner has said or accomplished for them. Not react at all when told they are loved. Start a contention to avoid their partner as much as possible. Remain too occupied to even think about having time for that love stuff. Deal with their partner yet don't let him or her consideration for them. Put their vitality into a hundred friendships yet don't let anybody, not by any means their partner, gets genuinely close. Disregard proclamations of love with an "uh-huh, that is nice" with-out genuinely feeling the love. Heft around feelings of hatred about how their partner has harmed them before, so they don't need to believe that the person loves them today. The uncertainty that their partner could genuinely love them since they don't generally love themselves.

Befuddle taking in love with feeling obligated to get things done for their partner—that is the point at which "I love you" gets mistaken for "No doubt, so what do you need from me now?" Play the "Truly, I hear you love me; however, do you incredibly love me?" game. There might be numerous reasons you experience difficulty saying yes to love. Family-of-origin issues. Despondent past relationships. Broken dreams. Whatever your reasons, one thing is sure: you have built up a habit of turning down opportunities to feel loved. You'd likely feel brilliant if you would let yourself express yes to love instead of no. This is what you can do to challenge that habit.

1) Imagine that the word no is written on an old familiar cap that you automatically go after each morning to put upon your head.

2) Now imagine that you've recently received a fresh out of the box new, adorable cap that says yes on it instead of no.

3) Your work is to make sure to put on the "yes" cap each morning. Likewise, continue checking during the day to check whether you've temporarily misplaced that new cap. If you can keep the "yes" cap on your head, you will be prepared to receive love when it is advertised.

4) Keep that "no" cap on the rack. In any case, don't stress over losing it. You'll generally have the option to take it to ease off the rack if you genuinely need it.

You have a choice each morning, evening, and evening about which cap to choose. What's more, believe us, it has a tremendous effect which one you pick. The "no" cap prompts isolation, defensiveness, loneliness, and dismissiveness. The "yes" cap prompts contact, warmth, and feeling loved. Here's your assignment: take one minute each morning to choose your cap for the afternoon. You can certainly pick your old familiar "no" cap if you desire. Simply make sure to explain to yourself precisely why you are doing that. Then again, you may decide to choose the "yes" cap. If in this way, at that point, keep it on your head. Think about what taking in love intends to you and recollect the entire day to give love access.

The five stages that let you take in love

It's one thing to need to take in love, however another to have the option to do as such. This exercise is designed to assist you with the real mechanics of receiving your partner's love, caring, regard, and admiration. Taking in love will be relatively simple if you follow this unmistakable and direct procedure. There are just five stages.

Stage One: Notice That Someone Is Showing You Love

Imagine that you've been walking in a mist. You were unable to see a lot of anything, yet now the mist is lifting. That is the point at which you notice someone approaching. It's your partner (or any other person who loves you). Your partner is saying something; however, you can't quite make out the words. You centre in a little, paying more attention until you can make them out: "I love you." Wow. You weren't expecting that, however there it is.

Congratulations! You've recently started the way toward taking in love. In any case, so far, all that is happened is that you've heard the words. You still need to do four new things to bring them into your heart truly.

Stage Two: Prepare to Take in Love

This is simply the point at which you quickly remind yourself that you need to take in that love. You prevent yourself from deflecting the love (by ignoring it, starting a fight, changing the subject, out of nowhere getting caught up with, running endlessly, and so on.). You dismiss any considerations like "I don't have the right to be loved" or "This can't be genuine." You centre around a specific something: permitting yourself to acknowledge being loved. You'll think something like, "My partner [or somebody else] is telling me I am loved. This time I'm prepared to feel it."

Stage Three: Receive Love

In this progression, you physically and intellectually take in your partner's love.

1) Breathe! Take a moderate, full breath. That lets your body feel loved.

2) Listen to those words with your entire mind, thoroughly attending to them.

3) Look directly at your partner's eyes so you can meet each other's spirits.

4) Relax. Taking love in is excellent, so you might also unwind instead of tensing up.

5) Feel the glow in your body. That is a physical reaction to the viewing of security that goes with taking in love.

6) Touch or hold the individual who loves you. That enables your entire body to feel loved.

7) Take your time. Feeling loved is one of life's great luxuries. So, don't surge off to do the dishes. Give that feeling of being loved drench access.

8) Believe in yourself and your partner. This truly is happening. You are being loved, right at this point. Take that love in.

Stage Four: Acknowledge That You Feel Loved

This progression is significant because you are validating what simply occurred. You do this in two different ways. The first is to let yourself know in your own words this idea: "I simply let myself feel loved. That felt _____." We trust the first word that rings a bell is "incredible" or "great." But it's alright if taking in love felt unnerving or weird or silly. Simply be straightforward with yourself.

The following method to recognize being loved is to express something for all to hear to your partner. You can express gratitude toward him or her. You can share your viewing reaction. Don't, however, automatically state "I love you" to your partner if saying that would distract you from your feelings. There will be a lot of time later to give some loving back. Recognize that your partner needs you to appreciate the experience of feeling loved, so you don't need to apologize or feel remorseful about being the recipient this time.

Stage Five: Accept That You Are Loved

This is the phosphorescence stage. You let yourself think about being loved. You notice your musings and feelings a couple of moments later, after an hour, a couple of hours after, the following day. You acknowledge that you are a loved person. You are both loved and adorable. What a miracle. What a trip. What an arrangement. It's in reality, evident. You are loved. Keep that feeling of being loved genuine in your mind, body, central core. That encourages you to prepare for whenever somebody discloses to you that you are loved. Take in love the slightest bit at once to avoid feeling overpowered the immediate feeling of being loved can be an immensely intense experience. Your partner says "I love you" and by one way or another you want to cry, your body tingles with vitality, you feel warm everywhere. You need to yell with satisfaction, give your partner an embrace or flee. A few people find it challenging to take in love at first since it feels overwhelming. A portion of these individuals may have felt covered by a parent or a partner before. Others mistakenly associate feeling loved with a feeling of obligation or guilt, as though being loved makes an obligation you should reimburse. Still, others have closed themselves down and are afraid to open up to love since they have been seriously harmed before. These individuals don't like the feeling of vulnerability that accompanies love. Finally, a few individuals avoid taking in love since they dread losing power over their feelings or actions. The shared factor for every one of these individuals is that they feel overwhelmed by love. The sensation of being loved is simply excessively startling, incredible, or intense. "Run," they state to themselves. "Hide. Escape from this viewing." And so, they run or hide. They ignore the remark, leave the room,

Make taking in love as a lot of a habit as brushing your teeth.

So, what would you be able to do if you are somebody who shies from the intense sensations of being loved? The appropriate response is to take in love a little bit at once. Attempt a nibble instead of a significant piece. Turn the music on most of the way instead of to the max. Light a flame to your heart yet not a five-hundred-watt bulb. That way, you can remain in charge. You won't get overwhelmed. You remain accountable for your mind and body. And yet you are learning better how to take in love. In the long run, you'll have the option to eat an entire supper instead of only one bite. You'll have the option to listen to more energetic music. You'll see the love in a more grounded light. Begin with, a simple objective: to take in your partner's love the slightest bit at once. So I don't get our meaning by taking in love the slightest bit at once? At the point when your partner says "I love you":

1)   It's alright to just look briefly at your partner, yet don't avoid all eye to eye connection.

2)   It's alright just briefly to reply ("Uh-huh, much obliged"), yet not to completely ignore your partner.

3)   It's alright to embrace your partner lightly, however not to stiffen against his or her touch.

4)   It's alright to leave in a minute, yet not to fastener out the

entryway.

5)   It's alright to state "I love you, as well," yet not all that quickly that you avoid feeling loved.

6)   It's alright to think about how anybody could ever need to love you, however not to decline to believe it.

7)   It's alright to inhale typically, however not to hold your breath.

8)   It's alright to notice your dread of taking in love, yet not to give in to it.

They're right there, waiting for you to watch. The espresso that is prepared for you when you wake up. That call just to make proper acquaintance while you are grinding away. A rental movie that is the sort you like most. Kind words. A playful address your arm. The additional time with the kids so you can finish your rest. Something special said or done during lovemaking that causes you to feel great. A little gift is given for reasons unknown. Every one of these things is your partner's method for saying "I think about you a ton, I need you to be cheerful, and I love you." Be that as it may, consider the possibility that you don't notice these gifts. Maybe you've never paid attention to such demonstrations of kindness and consideration. Or on the other hand, possibly of late, you're too bustling thinking about something else. Not noticing, you fail to recognize them or to thank your partner. That is no biggie when it happens now and again. Be that as it may, in the end, you will follow through on an overwhelming cost for your inattention. Unrewarded, your partner will begin cutting back on those kind words and deeds. It's five-year-old Joey's birthday festivity, in conclusion, he gets the chance to open up that gigantic present he's been looking at for the last week. Joey vigorously tears open the group—and a while later starts crying wildly. What was the arrangement? Taking everything into account, Joey had convinced himself that the group contained a bicycle and instead it held a PC structured distinctly for youngsters. Joey's people feel out and out terrible now. They were sure he would cherish that PC (regardless of the way that Joey had mentioned the bicycle on a couple of events and never referenced a PC). Father was especially disappointed considering the way that he cherishes PCs himself and wouldn't perceive any issues whatsoever accepting one as a present on his birthday. By and by he's getting angry with his youngster disliking the blessing and at himself for settling on an ill-advised decision. In the interim, Mom is thinking about whether they ought to re-establish the PC or demand that Joey make sense of how to use it.

There's a little Joey inside us all concerning feeling adored. That is the bit of us that knows correctly what we need from others. Exactly when we get the real blessing, we feel great. In any case, we feel awful when we are offered an improper blessing. In reality, the Joey inside all of us may even feel disliked when we get an improper blessing, thinking something like, "Sure, it's pleasant that she values my looks, anyway what I need most is to be acknowledged for how I think. I wish just once she'd state I offered a savvy remark."

Love is forgetting to keep track of who's winning.

Your first occupation, at that point, with this exercise is to notice the little manners by which your partner says "I love you." Your subsequent assignment is to recognize them with an unmistakable and direct "Bless your heart." Notice the Nice Things Your Partner Says and Does Right now, today, begin looking for all the beautiful things your partner says or accomplishes for you. (Try not to keep track of who's winning, however, so you can complain that there aren't sufficient or that you are doing more. Simply notice them.) Think of yourself as a telescope continually scanning the universe for signs of life, except you are seeking one select sort of life structure, in particular your partner's loving actions. Set your mind's telescope to "on" and keep it there. Recall that in the matter of love you will just find what you're looking for.

Say thanks to Your Partner for Those Nice Words and Actions

Begin thanking your partner for those kind words and acts. Try not to try too hard. A simple "thank you" is typically enough to tell your partner you've noticed what the individual has recently done. The most effective method to avoid the slide into defensiveness (just looking for the terrible stuff) We've mentioned before that we are marriage mentors. Tragically, it's frequently during couples' sessions that we get exercises on what turns out badly in relationships. We call one truly predictable example, the "slide into defensiveness." This slide happens when pained and anxious individuals begin watching just for their partner's criticisms, negative remarks, or different assaults. They are so worried about defending against the following assault that they remain on steady caution. They carry on like soldiers guarding the perimeter of their territory, ignoring anything that isn't threatening with the goal that their entire vitality can concentrate on survival. Sometimes these frightened soldiers even begin firing at shadows, convinced that the adversary must be out there. In any case, your partner isn't a foe soldier. * He or she isn't loading a weapon right now as you read this book. Your partner might be heading your way with a cold glass of lemonade or some tea intended only for you. Practice taking in love each time you give it out: Breathe in silver and inhale out gold A few peruses of this exercise manual may find it easier to give love than to receive it. Others might be only the opposite, happier with taking in love than giving it out. In any case, the vast majority feel best when they achieve harmony between these two reciprocal parts of human compassion. In this exercise, we describe a Buddhist way to deal with helping individuals discover and maintain balance in life. This exercise is particularly helpful as to balancing taking in and giving out love.

The Buddhists know and comprehend a great deal about breath and how breathing brings spirit into (inspires) the body, just as how breath and body fit into the universe. One school of Buddhist idea depends on compassion. There is a particular breathing exercise. This gathering of Buddhists likes to do. This exercise is designated "take in silver, inhale out gold." Both silver and gold are precious. In one manner, at that point, this exercise says: take in the best this world brings to the table, at that point, send it on as you breathe out to nourish and sustain others. So, think words like loved, loved, and cherished as you inhale, and as you breathe out, think words like loving, nurturing, and cherishing. First, you take in all the integrity of the universe, including the beautiful reality that you are loved. At that point, you return that decency, with your love, to the universe. First, you take in your partner's special love for you with each inhalation. At that point, you return that love as you breathe out. Both of you are enriched all the while. What preferred path over this could there be to show that the two parts of a loving relationship are as healthy as breathing?

Here are the directions for this valuable exercise.

1) Begin alone.

2) Decide which words you need to use as you inhale. You may pick silver, as in the first exercise. Love, sustained, cherished, or whatever other word that reminds you that you are

loved.

3)   Decide which words you will use as you breathe out: gold, loving, nurturing, cherishing, etc. These words will assist you with feeling love for your partner and the world.

4)   Take five to ten minutes per day to practice this breathing technique. Quietly inhale and breathe out, repeating the words you have picked. Try not to stress if your mind drifts off. That happens to everybody. Simply bring yourself back to these delicate words as you take in and out.

In the wake of doing this exercise for a couple of days, you might need to begin using it when you are with others. You may find this exercise particularly valuable now and again when you are starting to feel anxious, irritated, or upset. You and your partner might next have a go at doing this breathing exercise together. If you do, you might achieve a casual condition of shared lovingness with one another. Be that as it may, don't go into this exercise with expectations. Let whatever happens to be sufficient.

Take in love at your growing edge

Writers from the Gestalt school of treatment describe what they call a for each child's growing edge. They imagine that every individual is a little like a growing circular universe. Somewhere inside, at the focal point of the cosmic system, is your customary range of familiarity. This region is familiar to you. It has a sense of security. This is the place you keep all the habits of a lifetime. We include little anxiety inside this zone since it is sheltered. Route outside the safe place is the region of the obscure. You might state this is like the stargazer's idea of "dim issue." There's something out there right, something obscure and impossible to describe.

The total obscure fills individuals with unclear feelings of fear: "I don't have a clue about what's out there, and I don't know I need to find out." The most exciting piece of an individual's life is at the growing edge.

Metaphorically, this territory is at the edge of your usual range of familiarity, in the thin space between the safe and the dangerous, the familiar and the unfamiliar, the known and the obscure. Individuals feel excited when they arrive at their growing edge since they sense that here is the place; they can extend their feeling of being. The growing edge is a little frightening since you are venturing into new territory. Be that as it may, it's not terrifying because it's been within sight for some time. Here's a model. Sheila experienced childhood in a big city. In any case, she's been continuously drawn toward the outside. Once, quite a long while back, she considered simply chucking her city life, buying a ranch, and winging it. Right then since she figured she'd fail at farming. Also, Sheila was right at that time. She didn't realize enough to succeed. She signed up for some horticulture classes at the neighbourhood university, took a master gardening class, and started raising money crops on a little plot of land she leased from a close-by a rancher. She got a skilful. At that point, the rancher decided to retire. Sheila took a full breath and purchased his territory. She still doesn't have the foggiest idea whether she will succeed, yet she feels alright arranged to take the risk. She's at her growing edge in life, the spot between the known and the obscure.

You likely have growing edges in each significant aspect of your life. Take function, for instance. Indeed, there are parts of your activity you can nearly do in your rest. These are assignments within your customary range of familiarity. At that point, there are different things you would never plan to do because they are in your murky territory. Yet, finally, there are duties you are a little while ago beginning to handle. You haven't aced them yet, so they take a ton of thought and vitality. These new difficulties exist at your growing edge. They may raise your anxiety a bit, however without these new difficulties, work would, in the end, become quite dull.

Maybe you've arrived at a growing edge in your religious or spiritual life. The old explanations of the meaning of life don't feel quite right any-more. Dissatisfied with what's inside your customary range of familiarity, you may decide to evaluate a few new houses of worship in your denomination. Make another stride, maybe exploring another denomination or an increasingly individualized spirituality. You're not planning to change over to an entirely new religion, however. That would be path past your growing edge and into the obscure. We trust you have three particularly significant growing edges right at this point. These are in the zones of saying "I love you," showing your partner your love and taking in love. We'll concentrate on taking in love in this exercise. However, before we do that, if it's not too much trouble pause for a moment to address these questions:

1) How agreeable would you say you are saying "I love you" to your partner?

2) Are there any situations in which you can't imagine telling him or her about your love? (For instance, in public or during a contention. These are in your murky territory.)

3) Where is your growing edge—where you are merely learning to state "I love you" with your partner?

4) Can you name a few different ways you show the love that is well within your usual range of familiarity?

5)   Are there any ways your partner might want you to show him or her love that you can't imagine doing, at any rate not yet? These are in your obscure zone.

6)   How would you say you are starting to show love in more up to date ways? (These new endeavours on your part most likely feel a little cumbersome and startling up until now. In any case, you need to continue doing them until they become agreeable. These advancement zones are at your growing edge.)

Taking in love presents difficulties for pretty much everyone. That implies there are occasions and circumstances in which taking in your partner's love comes quickly and usually (when you are within your customary range of familiarity), at that point, there are likely times when you can't imagine taking in love (possibly when your partner is furious with you or when you are extremely occupied with something else). These situations exist in your obscure region. And afterwards, there are your growing edge opportunities situations in which you are merely learning how to take in your partner's love and caring.

Take in love and solace in any event, when you experience issues loving yourself, Therapists talk about how great guardians make a "holding environment" around their children. That implies the guardians are there when their children are harmed, dismal, or overpowered. All things considered; we adults can do something very similar for our partners. Your partner in life can assist you with feeling protected, warm, and, generally meaningful, loved when you are worried, hurting, angry, or dismal, or when you have lost confidence in yourself—however just if you let him or she do that for you. Perhaps at those times, you feel unlovable, yet that doesn't mean your partner needs to concur. The person in question realizes you merit loving. All things considered; your partner has decided to be your partner for some valid justifications. You've likely heard these sayings: "You can't give love to other people if you don't love yourself " and "You can just take in another's love to the degree you love yourself." There must be some fact to them, or individuals wouldn't rehash them as regularly as they do. Indeed, the young lady who reacts to her lover's "I love you" with "Goodness, how right? I do not merit loving" is taking in love just to the degree that she loves herself. Her lover's words make what's called cognitive dissonance between what she believes about herself ("I am unlovable") and what she hears ("You are loved").

A few people do believe they are unlovable. They may venture to such an extreme as to believe they are God's mistake—a complete failure of being. If you are like that, you will need to accomplish some close to homework so you can take in the love of the individuals around you. See our book Letting Go of Shame connect the feeling of being unlovable with the idea of disgrace. Notwithstanding, it would be a big mistake for you, or anyone using this book, to wait until you are "sound" and self-loving before taking in another's love. That is because taking in another's love makes feelings of self-esteem and self-esteem inside you.

Here's a typical model. One evening Mary is feeling particularly terrible about herself. She appears to have spoiled everything she's tried today: she did severely on a test at school, she committed a grave error at work, her kids disclosed to her she was mean since she wouldn't let them out of their errands, lastly, just to fill her heart with joy far and away more terrible, she broke one of her favourited espresso cups, spilling hot espresso all over her shirt all the while. Presently in strolls her partner, Charlie. "Hi," he says. "How's it hanging with you?" Mary dissolves into tears. "Terrible," she replies and enlightens him regarding her day. "Well," Charlie reacts, "I'm tragic for you that all that occurred. In any case, you realize I love you. Would I be able to give you an embrace?" So now what are Mary's options?

1.   She could push him away with a "Don't trouble, I do not merit loving" articulation. Result: They'll both feel isolated, and Mary's confidence will most likely drop through the floor.

2.   She could let him embrace her however continue telling herself she's such a failure, that he's a blockhead to love her. That way it appears as though she's taking in Charlie's love, however, she's genuinely not. Result: Charlie might believe things are better for some time. However, Mary's self-esteem will just get lower. She'll likewise be building deception into the relationship.

3.   She could graciously acknowledge the love that is offered by letting Char-lie embrace her while thinking something like, "OK. Regardless of how terrible a day I had; Charlie still loves me. Possibly I'm not such a horrible individual all things considered." Result: Mary does not just feel a little better about

Experience issues loving yourself:

Here's an exercise designed to assist you in doing two things:

(1) Discover the musings you have that make it difficult for you to receive your partner's love when you are discontent with yourself

(2) Assist you with changing those considerations to ones that will assist you with taking in his or her comforting love.

Act "as though" you believe individuals love you until you believe it the idea of acting "as though " originates from Alcoholics

Anonymous, where hesitant newcomers to the program were advised to go about as though they truly needed to remain calm. Individuals who act that route go to AA meetings, avoid bars, read the Big Book, find support, etc. The idea is that somebody doing these activities will continuously begin to like being calm. At that point, they'll go from acting "as though " to truly being in recuperation. Maybe you experience difficulty taking in your partner's love. If along these lines, at that point demonstration "as though " is a decent method to begin doing so. Here's a case of somebody who needs to act "as though." Recently we were having a couples counselling session with a lady we'll call Judy. Judy had endured numerous terrible misfortunes and treacheries when she was young. She had been maltreated and relinquished. Her folks had beaten her. To top it all off, Judy had been told again and again that no one could ever love her. She consumed these messages and developed into a grown-up who believed she was in a general sense unlovable. She at that point went into a series of awful relationships with mean, angry men. None of these men helped her vibe better about herself. They all contributed to Judy's belief that she was not deserving of love. By age forty, Judy wound up discouraged, dreadful, and desolate.

At that point, Paul went along. Paul was bashful, a man who had never had a serious relationship with a lady. He could be unrefined. He could be thought-less. He wasn't God's gift to ladies. Be that as it may, he was a decent man who was able to do genuinely loving a lady. Paul and Judy started dating. They committed. They married. That could have been the finish of the story. Carried them to counselling. Paul explained that he simply never felt that Judy indeed took in his love. Each time he said, "Judy, I love you" or anything like that she'd state something like, "No doubt, sure you do" or " Uh-huh; that is nice." Or she'd ignore him. Or then again perhaps she'd state, "I love you, as well, Paul" in a mechanical way that didn't feel quite right. Paul included that he was sure Judy loved him. That wasn't his anxiety. He just wished she could completely acknowledge his love.

We requested that Paul reveal to Judy he loved her. He did so and even explained the amount he appreciated her caring, how physically attractive he discovered her, the amount he making the most of her comical inclination. Judy heard his words. She looked as though she was trying to take them in. Be that as it may, always her head was moving horizontally, only a little, and unobtrusive path for her to reveal to us that she could barely handle it. "No, no," she said nonverbally. "I'm not adorable, so you can't love me." Also, she wouldn't take a gander at Paul while he was discussing. Avoiding eye to eye connection is an excellent route for Judy to shield from feeling associated with Paul. What would Judy be able to do so she can acknowledge Paul's love? That is the place acting "as though " comes in. Judy needs to change her behaviour to mirror the ways individuals who believe they are adorable act. That implies no head shaking or avoiding eye to eye connection. Instead, she needs to keep still while looking at him—that way, Judy allows herself to figure out how to take in Paul's love.

So shouldn't something be said about you? What amount would you say you are like Judy? Like her, do you have to act "as though " in request to figure out how to acknowledge being loved? Here is an exercise that will enable you to act "as though."

First, give yourself some time to see how others take in love. If your partner is acceptable at it, coolly let him know or her "I love you" and notice how the person in question takes it in. Watch others also—any individual who appears to be happy with receiving love, appreciation, and affection. Take in any event act "as though" you believe individuals love you until you believe it twenty-four to forty-eight hours just to accumulate information. Write down what you see here. The gap in the pail issue: Recognize and comprehend why you experience difficulty taking in love Sally and Larry have quite recently had intercourse. Great love. Caring love. That is when Sally goes to Larry and mumbles, "I love you with my entire existence." So, what does Larry say? "Nectar, that is extremely nice. I love you, as well." But what does he think? "I wish I can imagine how. I wish I could let myself feel loved. However, I just can't take in love."

Larry's by all account, not the only individual in the universe who experiences issues taking in love. He has a lot of organization, maybe including you. Larry experiences what we call the "gap in the container" issue. This is what that is like.

Simply put it in the container," we could state, and afterwards we could hold that love right where we could see it regularly.

Unnecessary pain. In any case, why endure when to be that as it may, consider the possibility that you can have a significant gap in it. Without a doubt, you could go up to individuals and request love. The love would fall right through the pail! At the point when you looked into that container, it would be vacant. You'd undoubtedly feel disappointed. You'd likely feel unloved. You might even feel unlovable. Perhaps you would begin believing that no one honestly thought about you. Finally, you might simply give up, deciding that you will never be loved. Notice, however, that the issue here is not with others. The opening in the basin is the issue. Others do love you. They continue putting love into the can. In any case, the pail doesn't hold that love long enough for you to feel it. Besides, it's your basin, no one else's. So the big question here is, how might you retouch you can so you can hold the love that individuals offer?

Stage One: Take Responsibility Now, in the Present, for Carrying Around a Damaged Bucket

It certainly would be interesting to see how your pail got harmed. That is the stuff of treatment, journaling, and challenging work. Yet, right now it doesn't generally make a difference how that basin got broken. That is because whatever happened can't be fixed. There simply is no magic answer in the past that will fix your love pail. So, the first step you have to take is to acknowledge sole responsibility for the condition of your container.

Stage Two: Gather the Equipment You'll Need to Fix Your Bucket

You'll require the emotional equivalents of a soldering iron, weld, and new metal. Select the action devices you'll require from the following list. Committing to take in my partner's love without doubting or questioning Gaining the mental fortitude to directly request my partner's love Learning the mechanics of taking in love ("Give your partner opportunities to be loving") Letting go of the past so I can take in love offered now Listening better so I can hear when others reveal to me they love me

Feeling confident that I merit loving

Reminding myself consistently that I genuinely am profoundly loved accepting progressively physical touch and holding without stiffening up visualizing myself having a repaired and overflowing love basin allowing myself to notice when I feel associated with my partner.

Stage Three: Fix the Bucket

This progression is the easiest of the three if you have arranged well. You've gathered your apparatuses, which implies you are completely arranged to retouch the basin. Presently you have to make a move. That implies utilizing each one of those devices today, tomorrow, and the following day. One approach to do so is to choose one device daily that you will focus on. Start with the most critical device from the list you simply made. If it's visualizing a retouched and overflowing love can, at that point today, a few times, take a couple of moments to visualize precisely that if it's committing to taking in your partner's love without doubting or questioning, do that, unequivocally and consciously. At that point, select another apparatus to utilize the following day. By selecting another apparatus every day, you will show signs of improvement at using them all.

The spiritual parts of taking in your partner's love

The word spirituality originates from a Latin expression meaning "to relax." Spirituality, at that point, implies a unique method for inhaling. We feel spiritual when we take in the universe and permit ourselves to feel profoundly associated with everything around us. That is the point at which we feel generally associated with God, ourselves, as well as other people. Breathing in the universe fills us with amazement, wonderment, happiness, and love. We sense during these minutes that there is God in each one and everything.

Furthermore, especially, we sense that there is a piece of God within our partner. We realize that our partner is special, superb, unique, and infinite. We praise that individual's existence at that point and become heartily appreciative that the person is in our life. This celebration of our partner makes spiritual intimacy possible. Genuine intimacy is spiritual. That is because intimacy involves two individuals giving and receiving each other's generally private, defenceless perspectives: their privileged insights, yearnings, expectations, and dreams. This kind of sharing changes oneself. An individual is never entirely the equivalent in the wake of having shared that profoundly of oneself with one's partner. The individual in question detects a colossal connection, a feeling of communion. Belonging takes on new meaning at this spiritual level. You are done walking down the way of life alone. Nor are you simply walking down the way of life besides your partner. Instead, you have brought your partner into your heart. You are walking down that way together, holding hands, until the end of time. Belonging like this is a healing experience. By feeling profoundly loved by our partner, we feel not so much disgrace but rather more love for ourselves. Accepting our partner without judgment encourages us to judge ourselves less also. We become some portion of an entire, creating a "us" that brings a feeling of completion, connection, and commitment. Spiritually united, we feel the infinite in the intimate and the intimate in the infinite. Taking in your partner's love at the spiritual level is always possible yet never simple. You should suspend judgment, criticism, and uncertainty for acknowledgement, celebration, and understanding. You are extremely, lucky to have this individual in your life.

The Expression of Intimacy

Passionate closeness and physical closeness are immovably related. Couples who have a better than average enthusiastic relationship furthermore, feel cherished and acknowledged have the best physical relationship. The accompanying inquiries were structured utilizing the definition of fondness as "any verbal or nonverbal articulation that conveys love in a non-sexual way." Friendship is, in no small degree, insightful expertise. Surely, even the people who seem, by all accounts, to be "naturals" here, for the most part, had some preparation in their adolescence as they saw and encountered the outflows of fondness exhibited around them. Those for whom fondness gives off an impression of being unwieldy may have started from a home where friendship was absent or then again on occasion conveyed. In any case, it's essential to talk about your childhood and how it has affected your desires here.

1) What does "fondness" mean to you?
2) How much fondness was there in your families growing up (verbal and nonverbal)?
3) How did you respond to the fondness (or nonappearance of warmth) you got?
4) How did your father show fondness?
5) How did your mother show fondness?
6) On the size of 1-10, what measure of friendship do you need in your marriage?

For Premarital Couples:

1) What was the demeanour toward sex in your family? Was it talked about?
2) Where did you get some answers concerning sex?
3) Have you revealed your sexual history to your accomplice? If not, why not?
4) Has nonappearance of love or sexual disappointment anytime been a factor for you in the detachment of a relationship?
5) Discuss your perspectives on sex diversion.
6) Have you talked about family arranging and also anti-conception medication?

For Married Couples:

1) What do you need in the solicitation to be in the air for sex?
2) Do you feel incredible starting sex? Why or why not?
3) How routinely would you like or envision sex?
4) How might you have the option to each adds to making your sexual relationship all the more fulfilling?

THE END

Made in the USA
Monee, IL
01 June 2020